AWAKENED WORSHIP

AWAKENED WORSHIP

Involving Laymen in Creative Worship

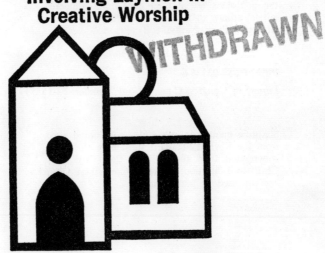

wilfred m. bailey

Abingdon Press
Nashville and New York

Awakened Worship

Copyright © 1972 by Abingdon Press

ISBN 0-687-02338-6

Library of Congress Catalog Card Number: 73-185543

Scripture quotations unless otherwise noted are
from the Revised Standard Version of the Bible,
copyrighted 1946 and 1952 by the Division of
Christian Education, National Council of Churches,
and are used by permission.

MANUFACTURED BY THE PARTHENON PRESS AT
NASHVILLE, TENNESSEE, UNITED STATES OF AMERICA

To the congregation of Casa View United Methodist Church

To the memory of Oscar E. Brown, Sr., who loved

Preface

The local congregation is quickly becoming the primary focus of concern to sensitive churchmen. Many of these same concerned persons are also becoming increasingly aware that worship is at the very center of the congregation's life and are sensing the tremendous significance of this fact. Worship in the local church, therefore, provides us with the prime channel through which we can and must proclaim the Christian faith to ourselves and to all we can reach.

If these words indicate that evangelism is at the heart of this book, then I have communicated clearly. I am constantly becoming more aware of that ever-present Activity in each person's life which offers him freedom to live, to love, and to minister to his neighbor. Along with this I experience deeper levels of awareness of the crying for such a Word from the sick and the healthy, the wealthy and poor, the powerful and the powerless. In the midst of both I see clearly the possibility of congregational liturgy, either to communicate or to pervert this faith.

The number of books offering new forms for worship steadily increases, and for this we can be most grateful. The concern with form and style is surely a valid concern. Yet it would be tragic if we assumed that the essential problem of worship in the church of today has to do with the contemporaneity of its forms. As important as forms are, surely of much greater importance is the character and quality of the Christian faith which is thereby given expression.

Two questions are imperative for Christian worship. Each question is a part of the other, but I am stating them separately. The first is, to what extent is the order of service consistent with the Christian faith? The second asks how well the Christian faith is communicated by that service. Both questions are basic to this book, and if they are taken with real seriousness, worship in our churches will be revolutionized.

What is true about worship, of course, is true about the total life of the church. Congregations making a real witness in the lives of members and of the world they touch are those who have committed themselves to a continuing search toward understanding in depth what the gospel of Jesus Christ is about. They have further committed themselves to the constant discovering of new ways of communicating this faith both in symbol and in society.

This is a great day for those who are serious about proclaiming the Good News of the gospel, who really are excited about life. We are most certainly in a state of flux in worship. But rather than this being an occasion for despair, it is a cause of rejoicing. This confusion is a gift of God, attacking our smugness, our casualness, and our absoluteness. We are now offered new possibilities that were not ours before. "Thanks be to God who has given us the gift of seeing that we do not know how to pray!" [1]

[1] National Student Movement, *The Wesley Orders of Common Prayer*, Edward Hobbs, ed. (Nashville: The Board of Education of The Methodist Church, 1957), p. 7.

Acknowledgments

In my first really serious questioning of worship it was Edward C. Hobbs who provided historical perspective, a rationale, and, most of all, his excitement about Christian worship. The few references to his contributions are really tokens of his presence in this book.

I am grateful to Fred D. Gealy, who acted as critic throughout the entire formation of these pages in the same manner in which he has sustained me throughout my ministry.

I am indebted to Lyle Schaller for his encouragement and insistence that my spoken words, experiences, and convictions about worship become a typewritten manuscript.

Bill McElvaney has contributed not only his personal support, but also his constant concern that liturgy be alive and communicative.

My thanks to Charles Cole, Tom Harris, James White, and Ed Sylvest for their critical reading of the early manuscript or portions of it. My special appreciation goes to Schubert Ogden for his careful and detailed reading of the entire final draft and for his very helpful and appropriate criticisms. Thanks also to Marge Lynn, who typed this entire manuscript in each of its many forms.

Contents

Introduction

The Awakening of Worship

Great ferment and excitement unequaled in our lifetime are bursting forth today in the services of worship of many congregations. This is true in almost every part of our nation, if not our world. We are not surprised to find youth responding to the variety of lively contemporary expressions so prevalent, but the youth have a large number of adults sharing their enthusiasm. One woman who identifies her life stage as "approaching elderly" says that after a half-century of faithful church attendance, she has for the first time been part of a service of worship that was "really alive."

These new forms and the renewed interest accompanying them have not reversed the overall decline in church attendance. They *have* caused rethinking among some church members about to become church dropouts and aroused new interest in others.

The changes also bring objections. A cabdriver complains to his priest, "I was really thrown by Mass last Sunday. I knock myself out all week trying to make enough money to feed my wife and nine kids. Then I show up on Sunday morning and find all those banners, balloons, and stuff. That isn't Mass; it's a party! What happened to Mass?"

Changes often bring crises in our lives, but worship changes have a special kind of explosiveness. One woman said that she was "devastated" when the long-used Apostles' Creed was replaced by the centuries-old but unfamiliar Nicene Creed one Sunday morning. Rational or historical explanations fail at such a time. This young adult knew only that someone had just knocked a big hunk out of the struc-

13

ture that she had leaned on so heavily each Sunday morning. It is not unusual for worship changes to be interpreted as clear signals that one's church has abandoned the true faith.

Other voices against revision are less despairing, but they regard the changes as failing to serve useful purposes and as making worship more difficult than ever. Some persons are not necessarily champions of past forms, but they cannot get excited about any of the new possibilities that have been offered to date. They agree that corrections are needed, but present revisions seem to them to miss the point of what worship is really about.

Many people are not moved one way or the other. They appreciated what has been and are about equally pleased with what has come. But whatever the response or lack of response, most are well aware that *changes are present* in almost every denomination in America today. Numbers of congregations have witnessed more worship changes in the past two or three years than in their previous total history. The changes in liturgy span a wide range. Some are timid attempts at injecting "modern flavor" into an otherwise highly predictable service that has been kept intact over a generation or longer. In contrast are those "happenings" in which most of the events come out of spontaneous responses that outwardly resemble little or nothing that the participants have experienced in a whole life of churchgoing. If a church is not involved in worship revision, it often finds itself unhappily involved in defending itself against liturgical change in some fashion.

Why has an hour that has meant boredom endured out of Christian duty to so many now turned out to be such an engaging experience, or why has a previously satisfactory and stabilizing service of worship become a threatening and frustrating occasion to others? A glance at our recent history of worship provides some help in answering these questions.

Relative Satisfaction and Then . . .

The scene is confusing. What happened to those good old days of a decade ago, more or less, when everyone *knew* what worship meant and could devote what little time was required simply to making it better? Until recently few people seriously questioned the services in which they participated. It is true that we had classified various congregations into "high" church or "low" church, but most wore their labels without embarrassment, even proudly. Few real questions of any depth were being asked within the local church, only occasional looks at hymns or evaluations of how smoothly things went on Sunday morning.

About eight years ago a group of fifteen Methodist pastors and laymen were asked why they followed the approach to worship they then employed. None responded immediately. Then one pastor shrugged, "I just follow the order of the church to which I am appointed." Another pastor said, "I always bring a service with me that I have come to over the years." A third said, "I take it out of the front of the Hymnal." Not one would try to offer a rationale for his particular order.

If we were severely lacking in knowledge about liturgy and if we were very fuzzy about the purpose of it all (and most of us were guilty on both counts), even more tragic was our euphoria. Laymen, pastors, and the church hierarchy assumed that everyone *knew* what Christian worship meant. At least we knew enough. We just needed to find better ways to make it more "effective" from time to time. Various administrative meetings were big in the post–World War II churches and great blocks of time were devoted to financial matters, promotion, and assignment of church school space, but scant consideration was given to the purpose and mission of worship. Area, state, and national meetings of denominations were giving little if any time to examining and pursuing basic questions related to that Sunday morning activity which claimed millions of man-hours. If worship was mentioned and comments were made, the attention usually centered on attendance, the "performance" of the choir, the sermon, and, in the more evangelical bodies, how many joined the church.

Some significant changes began occurring in worship two decades ago. They occurred in only a few local churches and only slightly more frequently in groups of pastors and student gatherings. Most of this "reform" came in those churches not following a prayer book. The push was basically an effort to dignify and "elevate" the service. It was not generally preceded or accompanied by theological ferment, but had, rather, a more aesthetic direction. Clerical collars, robes for the pastor (the choir already had them), more candles (51 percent beeswax), fewer Fanny Crosby hymns, a divided chancel, and more choral responses were the concerns found high on the priority list. But the direction began to shift in the middle and late 1950s away from these concerns.

Possibly the most damning aspect of these "early" efforts came in the form of a great concern to reform liturgy for the sake of liturgy. More recent awakenings in worship are a radical departure from this concern. They approach liturgy as an action necessary to members of the Christian community in order that the Word be made known to them and through them to all the world.

Why the Changes?

This deeper concern about worship began to appear in the middle and late 1950s. Most of those who began to raise the "new" questions and began to take action in their liturgy were also very much involved in the theological revolution that was making a definite impact. Paul Tillich, H. Richard Niebuhr, Reinhold Niebuhr, Rudolf Bultmann, and others were pointing many of us, inside and outside the seminaries, to a biblical theology that preceded changes in worship and in most major areas of a local church.

Secularization had an impact. Our society lets few segments of life go by without raising questions of meaning. We are often highly rational as a culture and demand rational explanations of worship with the same expectation that we display in other areas of our technological world. With a change in our relationships to authority and our regard for it, we are now far more likely to challenge those who put the service together, expert or not.

Surely the struggle for justice by racial groups, the effect of expressed changing values within youth, the Vietnam war, and other events in our total society have also had their impact on what happens in worship. Not to be overlooked, either, are the dynamics within the churches—ecumenical efforts, new administrative directions, etc.

Some of the worship changes of the middle and late 1950s appeared outwardly to be little different from those of the past, while others were obviously of another type. But the answers that were coming were secondary to a different kind of question that was being asked.

Different Questions—Different Answers

The kind of questions we ask make worlds of difference. Confusion and much fruitless argument often come from an assumption that we all are asking the same questions about worship. The big question we began asking was basic to all questions. We were not first wondering how much the service would be liked, how many people it would attract on Sunday morning, how many new members it would bring, or even how dignified or "beautiful" it might be. It was a "revival of concern in our time for adequate expression of the Christian faith in the action of worship."[1] We wanted to know how to put together and conduct a service that would proclaim the meaning of the gospel authentically to ourselves and to all who would hear. With this new question we received new answers and changes.

The past five years have probably brought more liturgy change than the previous fifty, even though many churches seem untouched. The difference is obvious between the return to the quite formal services of John Wesley by some Methodists and the present utilization of dance, banners, and guitars. At least some of these changes, however, are attempts to answer the same basic question that began to be visible a decade ago.

Where We Were and Where We Went for Help

Highly significant is the fact that some of us were attacked by the gnawing basic "why" questions during the "golden days" of church attendance. The congregation which I served was exhibiting larger crowds each successive Sunday at the multiple (two and even three) hours of worship. Questions which arise out of these conditions are radically different from those that come at a time of decreasing attendance. Instead of searching for answers to how we could build attendance, we were wrestling with the totally different puzzle of validity. What was happening among these expanding numbers who set aside almost one-half day of a valuable part of their week? Were we really involved in an act that was consistent with our calling to be the body of Christ?

If in those early days of concern about Sunday morning

[1] *The Wesley Orders of Common Prayer*, p. 5.

worship we had ventured a guess as to which communities would provide our new light, surely most would have looked toward the "free" churches—Methodist, Baptist, Presbyterian, Disciples, etc. We usually think of these as the highly flexible congregations. Churches such as Episcopalian, Lutheran, and Roman Catholic were obviously too wed to "canned" forms of the past ever to break out. And yet it was these very churches who had retained the traditional liturgy who gave the impetus to change.

Prayer Books and "Free" Churches

Our recent awakening in worship has not been the exclusive or even primary property of those churches whose liturgy is identifiable with past centuries. Some of these congregations and pastors have been the most rigid of all churchmen in their resistance to change. Faithfulness of our fathers is certainly no guarantee of faithfulness on our part. But the vital and exciting help received from several Episcopalians and Lutherans could come only from persons who had a sound grasp of the history of worship, as well as theological grounding.

Some of us have been quick to dismiss the "prayer book" churches as mortally fixed in their expressions and without flexibility. In truth, some of the most inflexible worship enacted takes place in the so-called informal or "free" congregations. The hymns, the announcements, prayers, sermons, altar calls, and the order itself has little or no variation from week to week. The primary difference usually found between the prayer book churches and the informal churches has been a matter of who put the services together and when they were formed.

The prayer book congregations have been employing words and forms developed over the centuries by rather large segments of the church. The extemporaneous or informal services are generally developed within the congregation or within a community only slightly less limited. The fixed form of the "extemporaneous" prayers can be seen in those used by a pastor who denounced "canned" prayers in favor of his own "prayers from the heart." One woman in that pastor's congregation knew his phrasing and organization, if not the exact wording, so well that she claimed to be able to predict within seconds at what point any of his prayers would end.

A friend of mine told me of a firsthand experience in liturgical renewal. He and his brothers were very interested in a decision on the part of their father, a Lutheran pastor in Germany, that the liturgy was too formal and lost on the people. They watched him throw off many of the prayers and forms of the Lutheran Church and write his own. Then they also watched these new forms become as fixed within their congregation as any of those he had dismissed and found the new ones to be just as noncommunicative.

It is important to affirm the responsibility of each congregation to work on its own services for its own day, even at the risk of a new rigidity. We know that one ancient form will not serve all churches at all times. We need to be reminded, however, that when we devise our own service, we not only face the possibility of a new inflexibility, but we often deceive ourselves into believing that we are still open and adaptable. We also often find that we have the additional problem of having a service which lacks centuries of community effort in its construction.

Pastors and laymen in churches with strong denominational prayer book orientation speak with disdain of the "experimental" churches. In truth, however, what service is not experimental? Are not the churches who have retained the forms and wordings of the past generation or more also experimenting to see if this will provide worship for our day? We are all experimenting today, some with new approaches, some with old, and most with both. Some recognize this fact and others do not.

To some of us it now seems quite reasonable that those churches steeped in the worship acts which were hammered out through the battles of centuries of the church's life should have had instruments that others of us lacked. But this lack of classical structures and forms that is so filled with dangers has also offered possibilities of more dramatic and obvious changes. Those with such meager heritage seemed to be on the forefront in confessing that we indeed did not know how to worship and were ready and eager to make sweeping changes. In retrospect we might say of the past ten or fifteen years that God used all of us, wherever we were, in his purpose to call the church to awakened worship.

This combined effort of many churches is illustrated by some Roman Catholics of recent years who eagerly talked with every Protestant who was alive in worship reform. They were openly seeking whatever knowledge and insights *anyone* could offer, without apology. Then they took all of this, sifted it carefully and fairly, and moved far beyond most Protestants. Now it has become even more an exchange between persons of all churches. The stronger our grasp becomes on the deeper meanings of Christian worship, the more we will denounce competitiveness and stereotypes of each other and will enter into a "rehearsal of the drama of our salvation." [2]

A Quick Look at the Range of Changes

The present worship hour of some churches involves so much change from past Sunday morning services that com-

[2] An expression of Edward Hobbs'.

21

parison is difficult. Instead of simply offering new wording of past forms, or even the substitution of a new prayer or new act of praise, a whole act or section sometimes has been omitted. The order in which such an act would have come is varied or completely redone. Not only have orders been changed, but *the very presence of any rational order is sometimes refuted.* At the center of these events have often been persons with years of church and worship experience.

Most changes are much less pronounced than the above. Some are basically no more than the reworking of wording of past centuries in order to correct misunderstandings, in the manner of new translations of the Bible. Such a simple move as the restoring of the congregation's "amen" after a reading of the Scriptures, a pastoral prayer, or the receiving of Holy Communion might constitute the bulk of change in some. Others involve somewhat major restructuring but are retentions of the basic forms.

Back to the Question

I have not intended to say that all of the changes in services of worship today have come out of a common understanding or that they are all attempting to answer the same question. They obviously are not. A common danger is to place all the services which have changed in one category and those remaining unchanged in a second classification. Then we can attack "their" side and support "ours." Or maybe we are unable to take sides because the conflict adds (or exposes) more confusion within us as to what worship is really about. Again, change or lack of change is not our first concern. Radical changes in churches sometimes provide or reflect little reawakening, while other churches can find exciting reawakening to worship within a traditional service.

Part I

The
Centrality
of
Worship

1

Worship: Reflecting and Shaping the Congregation

Worship is central to the life of a local church. We have no need to offer programs to *make* worship central. A person could not have been a Christian in the New Testament without worship,[1] and throughout the church's history a change in the liturgy has signaled a change in Christians' life-style.[2] To argue over whether worship is more important than evangelism, education, or other facets of the church's life is to miss the fullness of the gospel by attempting to make its many and varied manifestations compete with one another.

Worship is at the center of a church because liturgy (1) sets forth intentionally and unintentionally a portrait or proclamation of who that congregation is; and (2) helps shape that congregation's life. This chapter presents evidence and illustrations which indicate the basis of this claim.

Hey, Look Us Over

An outsider with some sensitivity and discernment could learn much about any particular congregation by attending its services of worship for several Sundays or even less. He could determine with some genuine clarity how that church understood evangelism, education, financial responsibility, missions, social concerns, the role of the minister, and the

[1] Gerhard Delling, *Worship in the New Testament* (Philadelphia: Westminster Press, 1962), p. xii.
[2] Dom Gregory Dix, *The Shape of the Liturgy* (London: Dacre Press, 1960), p. xii.

role of the laity. He would know also whether or not these people were sensitive to the world about them.

A church's open or closed attitude to present revelation, its basic trusts and fears, and the congregational belief in whether life is ultimately good will be signaled by what happens at worship. An awake observer would know from a church's liturgy how children, youth, and women were understood, and he would certainly see the congregation's basic theology.

The observer would know these characteristics, styles, and convictions not simply by listening to the sermon, telling as it might be. He would learn primarily by the manner in which the service is structured, what is included and excluded, and the degree and manner of participation by the total congregation. He could also determine much about the church's life by the presence or absence of certain visual symbols, by lightness or darkness, worn-out clocks and outdated posters, cleanliness, the type of seating, and an almost unlimited number of other messages.

One pastor tells how worship reflects vividly the two churches he serves. Through hymn-singing and responsive readings of the psalms, the characteristics are especially pronounced. Only about one half of the people in one congregation use their voices and then usually with little volume and a definite lack of unity. The other congregation, however, is almost unanimous in participation. These persons not only make themselves heard with strong voices but are also impressive because of their unison. The pastor sees pronounced parallels of the liturgy and the total congregational life of the two churches.

The first church is as apathetic in its approach to other areas of its existence as it is to worship. Contributions are spasmodic, members evidence little sense of community, and they generally indicate a lack of interest in serious study or evaluation of themselves as a church. The second church manifests enthusiasm, a willingness to assume responsibility, and the desire to work at common tasks with the same approach evidenced in its liturgy.

Similar stories are plentiful and would be expressed even more often if pastors and laymen were more attentive to how revealing their services of worship are. Our primary and most urgent concern is not first that of finding better services of worship, even though this is of vital importance. We can profit first of all by listening very carefully to what our present services and worship settings are telling us about ourselves.

Sex and Worship

The relationship of worship to the total life of a congregation is quite similar to the relationship of the sex act to marriage. If sex is separated from the other relationships of two people and is treated as the only important aspect, the marriage has serious problems. Likewise, if worship is considered to be the only major concern of a church and is unrelated to other areas of its life, that church is in trouble.

When sexual expression is missing in a marriage (assuming the couple is in good health), the husband and wife will probably lack genuine sharing in other areas also. In a similar way churches which give scant attention to worship are likely to have little else happening within them.

Sexual intercourse is similar to eating meals together, managing finances, and rearing children, in that all are parts of the marriage. Sex is also very different because more than any other activity, it reflects the depth with which the couple is relating to each other. Even if sex comes often but does not really involve acts of intimate expression and caring, the other experiences of the marriage are prob-

27

ably also lacking in a sharing of real depth. Worship, in much the same sense, is one among many work areas of a church, but it is also a unique area because it so well indicates how the congregation is involved through the week. Even if a congregation worships weekly but approaches the hour in a routine fashion, other church activities are also most likely approached without depth.

Reflection of their wider communities is not the only similarity of sex and worship; both similarly help shape community. Sex will not in itself provide a meaningful marriage, but if true intimacy is shared in sexual intercourse, the couple's complete life will be made richer in a way other experiences do not provide. When two people honestly and openly enter into the giving and receiving of physical love with genuine concern for each other, the community they have will be of a new level.

Worship, too, can change community. If the liturgy is solidly grounded in the gospel and if it communicates this gospel in clear acts, the rest of the congregational life will benefit. One church expresses this claim of worship by saying, "We will not initiate or allow to continue any program or activity in our church that is not shaped by the faith we proclaim each Sunday morning."

Coats, Ties, and Women's Hats

My friend Ted was told that he was living in a liberated age and was a member of a liberated congregation; he didn't have to wear a coat and tie to church anymore. His response was that he felt better and more appropriately dressed for worship with a coat and tie. He appreciated the liberation and would like for it to extend to his freedom to dress in the style that others were abandoning. I admit that I find real pleasure in seeing someone come to worship in casual

28

clothes, a nurse's uniform, or other "different" attire, but this is because it tells me that individuals know that no specific uniform-of-the-day is prescribed.

Who could seriously claim to determine that a church was stuffy if every man had on a coat and tie and each woman a hat? A person's vocation, his parents' dressing habits (whether he follows them or rebels against them), and other factors can determine what he wears to church. A man isn't a pietist simply because he wants to dress up on Sunday morning to go to the celebration. Others may prefer casual or sport clothes because they consider this attire best to fit special occasions.

Does the way a congregation dresses support the claim that worship is a reflection of the life of a congregation? The answer is "yes," but the meaning of what is worn has to be treated with more than a superficial look. Let the church reflect a position that this is a very significant time of the week and that each person is encouraged to express himself with whatever he believes to be appropriate for himself. Everyone dressed in the same style each Sunday morning might not tell us very much, but differences might well communicate that this is a people who honor one another's individual decisions. Respect of individuality in worship extends beyond the Sunday morning service.

The Case of the Black Nightgown

One five-year-old girl told her mother that she enjoyed worship in her weekday church school. When pressed for details, she reported in part that the preacher wore a black nightgown. Many adults in the free churches, pastors and laymen, have been less accepting of clerical garb. They feel that the minister has set himself apart and possibly above them when he appears in the service of worship wearing an

29

academic gown or clerical robe. These very reasons bring support from those clergymen who want to be set apart and from laymen who also welcome the separation, for whatever reasons.

Certainly there is validity in some of the above criticism, but liturgical garb—robes, stoles, etc.—can also reflect a seriousness about worship. The robe might well say that the pastor recognizes that he has been ordained for his role by the church. He doesn't lead the service because he is a man of more faith, or smarter, or any other such justification. His "uniform" tells that the pastor has been ordained by the church to function in this particular leadership capacity. A robe can help the congregation make a wide identification with the universal church. It can help direct attention away from personality and can be a humbling reminder to a would-be prima donna.

The robe can say to the laity that beyond the service of worship, this pastor can be trusted in counseling to assume a professional stance. A pastor who knows that he is not morally superior or set above laymen, and that he serves laymen who know this, is not likely to have much of a problem with a robe. Unlike the pastor who was embarrassed about distributing Communion elements (who am *I* to be giving *them* the body of Christ?), the one who knows that he has been appointed by the whole church to this functional office may find the putting on of the robe each Sunday morning to be an assuming of the historical office which calls him to more serious service. Some of us are still experiencing this after a considerable number of years.

High and Lifted Up

Reading the Scriptures and preaching from a pulpit draws much of the same criticism as does the robe and has much of the same to commend it. The psychiatrist who sees the massive and elevated pulpit as a stage prop to put the preacher above and beyond the reach of the worshiper could well be correct about one of its possible functions. For the pastor to dismiss the pulpit and to stand among the people can also be interpreted as an arrogant kind of "Look at me; I'm willing to act *as if* I'm as lowly as you are." Neither pulpit nor lack of one will guarantee that we don't communicate a superiority attitude. This is an individual problem. A pulpit can, however, help indicate the kind of seriousness with which a particular church treats these "Thus saith the Lord" acts—the sermon and the Bible lessons.

We all know that the pastor sees and understands only in part, and if *he* doesn't know it, the situation will profit little by liturgical adjustments. Introductions to the Scripture readings need no acknowledgment of how these words might not be the exact words that Jesus spoke. We can handle that in the education classes. And sermons need a minimum of "my opinion is" interjections. The listener will seldom suspect that the minister has a hot-line by which he receives absolute information. Why not let the pulpit, the robe, and any other objects help tell the congregation that the service is indeed a most serious proclamation of that Word through which we receive life? The other side of the coin—the temporality of the proclaimer—is quite obvious. Let the service of worship say to all that this is a congregation which understands itself to be charged with a commitment to God's redeeming work as it comes to us through the historic church of Jesus Christ.

Blunders and Goofs

The layman who drops the offering plate and the pastor who forgets the Apostles' Creed seldom see their embarrassing acts as contributions to a service of worship. But have you ever been in a service that seemed so perfectly planned and executed that you would have welcomed a blunder, especially on the part of someone else? You could almost interpret such an act as having been sent by the Lord.

The "too perfect" service and the response we make to mistakes are most important to our theme of how services of worship reflect the theology, overall understanding, and life of a congregation. This is not a plea for planned mistakes in order to give a service the human touch. The acceptance of blunders or goofs as inevitable, however, and the response of a congregation to them can be a real gospel proclamation.

Weddings, which are considered by many of us to be an occasion of worship in the church, offer an excellent illustration of the intense concern some have that no mistakes be made. Brides are often nervous, of course, but one woman who was especially uncertain about it all came to me almost daily for reassurance that nothing would go "wrong" at her wedding which we were planning. A friend of hers had been humiliated when the pastor slipped and said, "Do you take this man to be your wedded wife?" Would this happen to her? Would I possibly drop the ring? Her exaggerated worries reflect the fears of other brides and highlight a too-common belief that an entire service, whether it be a wedding, baptism, or regular Sunday morning order, will fail if somebody stumbles.

By all means let's not excuse sloppy and haphazard preparation. Continued mispronouncing of biblical names and places might ease by most members of a congregation, but pastors know they are cheating if they don't use a recognizable Bible dictionary to check out words about which they are uncertain. Musicians, choir members, and others who have leadership responsibility communicate a lack of full or serious commitment to the Christian faith when their inadequate planning or casual rehearsals constantly show through. To acknowledge that we can worship God in *any* service is no excuse for careless, slipshod efforts, and these paragraphs are in no way intended to encourage or accept a nonchalance about worship. Having made as much of preparation time as we believe to be in keeping with other claims on us, however, we then can accept ourselves as creatures who will be subject to errors. The way we respond to them will probably tell the congregation more about our understanding of our creatureliness than would a series of sermons.

Few members were offended when the pastor smilingly announced after the closing hymn, "Anyone who would like is invited to remain after the benediction and sing the hymn I forgot to include during the middle of the service." The temptation might be to keep silent and respond to any who mention the omission, "We were running close on time and I chose to eliminate it." Few excuses would seem plausible for dropping the offering plates, and explanations and a forced cover-up humor are not required. Some pastors and congregations have learned to laugh at themselves on occasions. They recognize that the One whom they worship is perfect but that they are not, and neither are the forms they use. These persons will find appropriate expressions or style to make known their acceptance of imperfection when mistakes come.

The significance of this concern for honest and accepting responses to blunders is all too likely to be minimized, but the manner of response to an error can communicate more than the nineteen minutes of well-prepared preaching which preceded it. Our prayers and our sermons might have been aimed at our need to confess our true selves, to be able to

accept ourselves as God accepts us, but how great a procla
mation when this is said through our action!

Can We Be "Too Perfect"?

As mentioned earlier, we sometimes would welcome a
mistake because we say that the service is just "too perfect."
Our real complaint is not likely to be that a service is too
well planned, but that it lacks spontaneity and humaneness,
or warmth. Maybe we simply find the worship too mechani-
cal. Careful planning doesn't necessarily produce impersonal
services. On the contrary, with enough forethought we can
plan and design services that are far more likely to involve
the congregation than those in which we come together and
wait for something to happen or try to be folksy.

2

The Role of Physical Settings

Christians are grateful for the world about them. Our gospel proclaims that God acts through his creation, namely, this material world in which we live. Worship always has a setting whether it is a grassy hillside, a tornado-devastated area, or a great cathedral. For most of us it is our local church building. The exteriors, interiors, and furnishings of these buildings are constantly informing viewers and participants about the congregation. Here is a look at the message of the settings and their function in reflecting and shaping a congregation's life.

Architecture Tells Others About Us

Church buildings considered individually often tell us little and sometimes even mislead us in our picture of a certain congregation's understanding of itself. Church structures on a nationwide basis, however, communicate very vividly what we as a total church have believed about ourselves. Here and there in various cities, towns, and open country we are struck by an excellent church building. It commands our attention. Without giving the impression of being flashy or fancy, the building conveys strength, interest, aliveness, the presence of a distinct community, and it points beyond itself. It seems to be a part of the world about it, interacting with it, but still not swallowed up by its surroundings.

For each of these architectural surprises, however, we find a number of church buildings that tell quite a different story. We see dreary colors, poor imitation stone siding, and efforts to duplicate colonial structures which are no different from the service station or supermarket down the block. Modern concrete and steel have been disguised in an attempt to recall the magnificent Gothic cathedrals of another century. Lines are made in the steel-reinforced concrete to give the impression of stone vaults and arches. Bland structures are often embellished with nonfunctional imitations of the flying buttresses and storm shutters which were so much a part of past buildings.

These structures which form the overwhelming majority of our church housing today are saying bad things about the church. They tell of an unwillingness to participate in today's world where people are being born, bleed, have happy times, become lonely, find fulfillment, and in which they die. We see no indication of risk. One person says that the imitation Gothic is often appropriate architecture. It can tell of a congregation that is really held together internally by the technology and value systems of today while trying desperately to devise an exterior covering which will identify it with a past age that surely must have been grounded in the faith.

Some buildings are most certainly twentieth-century glass and steel but seem to exhaust themselves in an effort to shout, "Look how modern and relevant we are!" Viewers see shallowness and the absence of any grounding. The effort to attract attention comes across as the most urgent concern of those inside.

A particular congregation's life is not necessarily revealed by the exterior of its buildings. Most of us know far too many contradictions in building appearance compared with congregational life. Most exteriors reflect the orientation of one pastor or at most a building committee and pastor at one specific point in the church's history. And since deciding about buildings is such an occasional event in a church's life, the decisions that are made often come without very wide consideration of alternatives. Congregations can certainly wither away in fine buildings, and reawakenings most certainly can come about in the deadest of housing.

Nevertheless, an overall look at the buildings that house our worship tells us much about the church as a whole. If what these buildings say is wrong, some significant but relatively inexpensive changes can help alter the message which we send out through our wood, stone, steel, and through the grounds which surround the buildings. Changes can bring a new word to those outside and the future of the congregations inside can be reshaped. One saying is that we shape our buildings and what we shape then shapes us.

The Inside Story

Far more important and communicative to the congregation and those who visit a service is what the inside of a building says. We have heard and read reports by various institutions of fantastic changes of relationships that take place through attention to arrangements of seating, lighting, colors, and other visual, audio, and tactile considerations. Our churches have indicated little seriousness about this kind of information. I am not speaking of manipulative gimmicks, but rather of a concern for the whole person and not his intellect only.

What is the inside story of our churches? Do they convey a recognition of man's total life? Color is a good means of pursuing this question. Whether colors come to us primarily through inner-city neon, billboards, signal lights, or through the far more exciting and fulfilling sights of sea, forests, fall leaves, grass, flowers, and sky, those of us who are gifted with sight live in a world of color. Our church interiors can communicate a recognition of this fact in our effort to proclaim the gospel in its richest terms.

What does our seating arrangement tell about the relationship we have with one another? Are we rigidly fixed forever in one manner of seating, usually all facing forward? We have heard much criticism of lining people in rows in which our basic view of other worshipers is the back of their heads. Such criticism has been needed. The very dominant spectator attitude about worship has undoubtedly been helped along by such an arrangement, but the solution is not so simple as moving to the "correct" design of having the congregation in a circular or semicircular style. A friend once expressed his response of shallow chumminess in witnessing a circular-oriented group singing "They'll Know We Are Christians by Our Love." The group's message to him was one of a primary concern and exaltation of themselves, a turned-inward approach that rejected any transcendence. Semicircular seating, even with its problems, does provide a quite workable and helpful arrangement. It offers the advantages of bringing the congregation closer together, provides a better relationship to the altar-table and pulpit, and enables members to proclaim the liturgy to each other face to face.

Two Reminders

Necessary to the above considerations and the ones that follow is a reminder to ourselves that we will most certainly not find liturgy and physical arrangements that will present one true message and present that message to one hundred percent of the people. We hedge if we say that our efforts might be misunderstood. They *will* be misunderstood by some, including in part each of us who works on them.

The danger of evaluating our work primarily in terms of what feeling or mood we provide is the second reminder.

Our task is not that of providing settings which manipulate the emotions of the worshiper, although we certainly do not reject the validity and importance of feelings, mood, or emotions of people. Searching for broader and more inclusive ways to communicate with a person's whole being is not synonymous with efforts to manipulate emotions. Expanding the areas of communication beyond the verbal could well bring more emotional involvement and response. It is no more our purpose to prevent this than to create it. Christian worship is not aimed at producing laughs, tears, fears, or warm feelings, but it receives them all if they come.

Is It for Real?

A clergyman friend of mine was being shown around a new and expensive building. As they approached the pulpit, he stopped to look at the vines and greenery that poured out of a giant container. The member realized how closely my friend was examining the "ivy" and quickly reassured him, "The green plants are imitation, but they are more expensive than the real ones!" What do our places of worship communicate in authenticity?

Authenticity is no magic word. We would be the losers, for example, if we could not have a print of a masterpiece. Even though we realize the inferiority of prints compared to the originals, these paintings simply aren't available to most of us. We work within certain limitations without need for embarrassment. Authenticity asks whether we use what we have in a way that is designed to deceive. Some of us can genuinely appreciate large paper flowers which are intended to come across for just what they are—paper and handmade expressions of flowers. More questionable, however, is the wax fruit that proves itself to the degree that you are tempted to take a bite out of one of the apples.

The equating of costliness with quality is the second concern to come out of the story of the imitation green plant. We have accepted in varying degrees the belief that the more money we pay for an object, the greater is its quality. Congregations who want to improve their places of worship but have no funds often find that much of the needed resources are already theirs. Not able to purchase pulpit falls or other paraments, they decide to make them almost totally from materials they have within their own homes. When these efforts have been approached with care and serious study, the results have often far exceeded most of the paraments that might have been bought and have had their own particular value. The many creative ways in which the materials can be put together without a person's being in any way a seamstress and the imaginative work of first-time amateur designers encourage others to enter in.

Gold Crosses and Hungry People

Few complaints about the church are louder and few are voiced more often than those which condemn the church for spending millions of dollars on fine buildings and luxurious appointments while people in the world around it suffer from hunger. How disturbing it is to see the glistening gold steeple of a cathedral rising out of a neighborhood of deplorable housing conditions. The cry, of course, is that the church should be spending that money on the poor instead of wasting it on extravagant places of worship. Is God not more concerned about one hungry child than about a fancy altar? The answer to that question is simple and obvious. Relating this concern to all expenditures on the setting for worship is not so simple. Where is the point at which money spent on sanctuaries should cease?

If a congregation must spend a major portion of its time

and energies trying to raise funds to keep up payments on its buildings and other possessions, we might see quite clearly a need to sell all (well, part of it at least) that we have and give it to the poor. But what of churches who are devoting a very sizable portion of their common life to visiting those in prison, feeding the hungry, etc.? Is there ever a penny that could not and should not be used for the needy?

One preliminary response is to question the nonchurch complainer on how he can so self-righteously damn the church for not feeding the hungry while he is usually offering no help to those in need. His rationalization that he, at least, doesn't pretend to be "good" is a poor defense. But then that is his problem, and the church still must deal with its problem.

At least two responses must be made to money spent on and in church buildings as related to continued need and starvation surrounding us. The first is a realization that we shall always be somewhat uneasy about any internal expenditure by the church, and that is as it should be. We can never become really comfortable in our actions or dismiss the tension that will always be experienced by Christians when someone is hurting.

We deny our creatureliness and we strive for self-justification when we attempt to proclaim a formula that will prescribe the proper amount or proportion of funds that can be directed to the congregation's own life. We must always remain sensitive to any judgment or acclaim, knowing that either can well be the judgment of God. But creatures need not be embarrassed about creaturely decisions. That's the Good News. We make our decisions and boldly live with them as long as they are consistent with our understanding of the faith.

Consider, secondly, how condemnations of expenditures on liturgical items, set over against physical needs of the neighbor, can also be a perverted word about life. With all of its obvious demand on serving each other through what we commonly call social action, the New Testament leaves no question about the presence of a greater dimension to life. The tendency to talk superficially about the "spiritual part" of life has blurred and distorted what Christ is telling us. We are not told to meet a person's physical needs and later meet his needs of the Spirit.

The division is a lie. Much of what passes as orthodox, true-to-the-faith, and fundamental Christian truth is really a reduction of the concept of living in the Spirit. We make "life in the Spirit" one section among other sections of reality, even though we champion it as the most important section. The demand of the gospel is that every section of life, every act of life, be done in the Spirit. As those who live in the Spirit, we are called to understand and relate all that we do—social action, worship, and all else—as part of a life that always offers joy to each human being without qualification.

Is Not Life More Than Food?

Will the gift of food to the hungry give that man life? Life is rejected constantly by people with stomachs containing plentiful supplies of healthful foods. Will a warm coat provide life's depth and fulfillment for the shivering and ill-clad beggar? Fine woolen sweaters daily warm the bodies of persons who approach each new day as a sentence to be served. How insulting we are to a man when we reduce his meaning to physical needs! How we deny our own experience and the experience of those we know!

Jesus never minimized the necessity of providing for physical needs, but he never denied the whole of life by reducing it to include only this area. If we believe that any human being is denied the total meaning of life if *we* do not give him food to eat, then we believe that the cross is a hoax. Certainly we are not willing to say that God cannot provide in all situations or that our apathy can thwart God's gift of life. Our failure to act certainly does prevent life, but it is *we* who die because of our inaction. We provide food because a man is hungry. We fail him and ourselves if we attempt to represent the act as assuring him life.

What a sellout of life when the church apologizes for *every* investment in liturgy! The church's services of worship are the primary events through which the transforming Word is made understandable to some in the most tragic events they experience. We need simply to look about us to see that the man with his physical needs supplied is no less separated from the gift of life than is the deprived ghetto-dweller. This must not be interpreted at all as discounting the importance of food, education, etc., but if our worship proclaims man as living by bread alone, it has betrayed the one who feeds, the one who is fed, and the gospel of Jesus Christ.

Already in the mind of some readers is this New Testament story:

And while he was at Bethany in the house of Simon the leper, as he sat at table, a woman came with an alabaster jar of ointment of pure nard, very costly, and she broke the jar and poured it over his head. But there were some who said to themselves indignantly, "Why was the ointment thus wasted? For this ointment might have been sold for more than three hundred denarii, and given to the poor." And they reproached her. But Jesus said, "Let her alone; why do you trouble her? She has done a beautiful thing to me. For you always have the poor with you, and whenever you will, you can do good to them; but you will not always have me. She has done what she could; she has anointed my body beforehand for burying. And truly, I say to you, wherever the gospel is preached in the whole

world, what she has done will be told in memory of her."
(Mark 14:3-9)

These words of criticism against Jesus and the woman
were probably the expression of far deeper resentments and
hostilities than the matter of "wasted" ointment. The critics
were not likely to have been putting forth a claim for the
poor. Likewise, contemporary persons who use Jesus' reply
as encouragement of apathy toward the needs of people in
terms of hunger, clothing, etc., grossly pervert the gospel
message and offer a most unreasonably narrow interpretation of the Scriptures. This passage proclaims to us the
vital role of those dimensions of life which are not ex-
hausted by the physical.

Quality, Luxury, and Sin

The church has the task of deciding the quality of what
it purchases and/or creates. The tension is always present.
Shabby settings can say that worship is not taken seriously
or that it is not worth much investment. A concern for
quality, on the other hand, can come to be regarded by the
worshiper as indulgence in luxury. The next step is to give
this "indulgence" the name of "sin." We need no material
guideline. We give thanks to God for our freedom, awe-
some as it is, and concern ourselves with how the church
best ministers to people, all people. We are not asking
how the church can give people what they like or primarily
what makes them feel good. We are determining from the
perspective of the Christian faith what it means for a
specific congregation to fulfill its mission to the world. The
world, of course, includes its own neighborhood and fellow
members and extends to all. Our decisions about investment
in liturgy—paraments, silver, linen—are a part of the total

44

question of being the body of Christ and are treated no more and no less seriously.

Beyond the Eye

Individual senses cannot be isolated, but most of our attention so far has been basically visual. Sound counts also. Not being able to hear what is being said in a service of worship can be painfully distracting and frustrating. Poor acoustics in a building can make us feel that we really needn't bother paying attention. If what is being said is important, it would be audible.

"Don't worry about me," says the preacher. "I can shout loud enough to be heard by everyone." Heard? Yes. But the limitations of near-maximum volume prevent wide possibilities the voice can offer in communicating. Bad acoustics convince some that the church doesn't take its worship very seriously; its proclamation just isn't as important as that of movies, television, or radio in which great care is exercised to "come through." Alterations which increase or decrease the aliveness of a room or the use of quality amplification are not extravagance. We cannot afford to pay salaries, mortgages, utilities, and upkeep on a building for worship in which communications are not clear.

Without necessarily advocating plans of sending "religious" odors into the room, we still must concern ourselves with other senses, including odors. Does our church have a distinctive odor? If so, the primary question is an awareness on our part of what it is—floor wax, flowers (plastic or real), a general mustiness, or a number of combinations. What does this odor mean to the worshiper? It must be in keeping with the whole service.

Are we getting too picky to talk about odors? Our lives respond much more quickly to odors than to words. A senior high boy realized that he was being distracted and disturbed by an odor in the church office. The source was a bottle of stencil correction fluid and the cause of trouble, he soon realized, was the odor's resemblance to what he smelled in his doctor's office. On a recent occasion my wife quickly backed away when she smelled a different tooth powder we had purchased. When she consciously identified the odor with some medicine she had taken during a serious childhood illness, her anxiety lessened. We would do well to reconsider our criticisms of incense.

Sights, sounds, odors, and other sensations produce various responses with each individual. I am in no way calling for a search for stimuli to bring about "religious feelings" or for those which will be inoffensive to all. This is neither possible nor is it our aim. We must, however, become more sensitive to the fact that the room in which our worship takes place is sending out many messages. Those who take worship seriously will be conscious of these and take responsibility for their part in the lives of those who worship.

The relationship of the congregation-at-worship with the world outside is one of the many other considerations of the worship setting. Can we see any of the trees, sky, or outside light? Viewing traffic or activities outside the window can be quite distracting. Some indication of the continuing world around us, however, might indicate that we are those who have come "out" of the world (symbolically) to hear and proclaim what it means to be alive as disciples of Christ "in" the whole world.

Consideration of the building, furnishings, and total environment could include temperature and a very long list of other details. The particular areas presented in this chapter represent the major concerns for which the church must take responsibility.

3

A Message Through People

Liturgy is primarily action. We move, therefore, from what surrounds us and direct our concern to what we reflect by what we do in worship. What is communicated about us and to us by the manner and style in which we enter into or fail to enter into the service of worship? We can and certainly should examine the words of prayers and sermons, but our primary concern here is not verbal. Our present purpose is to look at the less intentional or less conscious communications. These can be the most powerful ones. The point is made by the story of the two contrasting churches which was given in Chapter 1.

What About Laymen?

The entire third part of this book is concerned with the involvement of laymen, but we must raise the question at this point as to the degree to which laymen have a real voice within a particular church. The liturgy will tell us. If the service is obviously the pastor's "show" all the way, then we might well suspect that most of the other areas of the church's life will also exclude serious participation by the laity. This is not to minimize the pastor's need to provide strong leadership in worship, administration, and other expressions of the church's witness. Few acts are as revealing, however, of the pastor-superior attitude as is the clergyman exercising a stranglehold on worship. Some services are, in fact, out-and-out insults to lay intelligence.

"This morning's hymn is to be found on page thirty-five

in your hymnal." Most bulletins have listed the hymn number and members, of course, know that the likely location for the hymn is the hymnal. Then the pastor signals with his arms that the congregation is to stand. He offers these instructions even though the people in that church have stood for the singing of the opening hymn for seventeen years and even though instructions to stand are indicated in the printed order.

We may become somewhat accustomed to this approach, but it can be annoying even though no direct insult is intended. Of a more serious nature, like other signals from our worship, it tells of a probable lay-clergy relationship overall that is a handicap to the church's mission. Does the congregation wait for the pastor to give repetitive signals for other action? Will the paint continue to peel before laymen's eyes until the pastor initiates a painting party? Will bills go unpaid until the pastor calls for money to be secured or checks written? A laity that assumes responsibilities in these areas is unlikely to long endure the hymn announcements described above.

The pastor's regard for himself and for the laity might also be indicated by the incident. Does the pastor regard himself as the final word on scriptural interpretation, the only judge of theological and ethical questions? Even more crucial, does he believe that he is infallible in administrative judgments? Further, does the congregation regard him as such or at least allow him to perform such a role?

The pastor who conveys a reasonable regard for the congregation's intelligence and their initiative may be battling against years of "dumbed-down" language, but his approach can relay to the membership his respect for them. This expressed confidence could also give the word to laymen that other avenues of ministry are open for them to enter and exercise their abilities.

48

Treating Youth as if They Were People

What role do the youth have in Sunday's worship? Ordinarily we can describe their part rather quickly. They usher on "Youth Day." If they are sufficient in number and the music program is extensive enough, a youth choir may be included in the service on special or periodic occasions. Or maybe they don't have any responsibility.

The amount of exposure youth have in worship is less important than is the type of service they have been called upon to do. Even if they handled all the ushering every Sunday morning, this activity could vividly illustrate a church's almost standard practice of keeping youth within self-contained areas. What a different story might be set forth if youth participated in worship tasks that are shared with adults and children. They can usher and they can also bring the Communion elements forward (where "bringing forward" is the practice), and they can assume "people" parts in the liturgy rather than "youth" parts.

We are indebted to youth for the contribution they have made through music in recent years. Most churches who have wanted to "go contemporary" in worship have sent for the youth and their guitars, and young people have certainly increased the power of many services by their special gifts. These gifts, however, can be so much more inclusive. What these teenagers do and don't do in the whole hour of worship indicates generally the adults' view and treatment of them in the church's total life. They have been isolated too long in their own structures, organizations, and by their musical contributions. The clues as to how we are regarding them will come from how the youth are involved in the Sunday morning liturgy.

49

Do We Suffer Little Children?

Our considerations about youth and worship are in some ways basically similar to considerations about any other age group, including children. Each group, however, also has its own specific questions. Should children receive Holy Communion before they are confirmed? At what age should parents bring them to services of worship? Some local churches have these questions answered for them by their identity with a denomination and others have probably solved some of these kinds of problems on their own, at least to their satisfaction. Most of us, however, find that such questions just don't answer easily and that they even defy very sharp answers. Our wrestling with these decisions and the manifestations of this wrestling that appear in worship tell us more about ourselves than we ever suspected.

Children will not remember many of the words that were spoken during their early times at worship, but they will have the Sunday morning experiences with them throughout their lives. If their parents, the congregation, and the clergy communicated love and acceptance to them or if they received only signals of tolerance at best, the message will be a lasting one. The congregation that requires confirmation or at least a certain age for those receiving Communion might well communicate that it is careful about its sacraments. It runs a possibly greater risk, however, by telling children that they are not included. This reasoning will break down if pushed to its ultimate, but, as a friend of mine says, "I don't like to push anything to its ultimate."

The argument is basically consistent. We don't prohibit boys and girls from listening to sermons that they can't comprehend or from hearing or saying creeds that make no sense to them. Their inclusion as those who receive the elements of Holy Communion along with their parents might be one of the most important acts of worship. As they grow older, maybe they will grow in their knowledge of what the Eucharist means. Maybe their parents and the pastor will also grow in an understanding of what it means. That is one of the prayers of the church.

Prior to the question of the appropriate age for receiving the elements is the concern about a proper age for children to be present in a service of worship. A child crying, or the busy work of a mother attempting to keep the preschooler in his seat until the benediction, causes distraction regardless of how cute the child is. One professional advice-giver told an inquiring parent to keep a noisy child out of the service in respect for the amount of time the pastor had spent in preparation of his sermon. People, including children, are not made for sermons. Sermons are made for people, including children.

We can be sympathetic to the limitations of a child's interest span and comprehension capacity without disregarding the effect of talk and play on the nearby bachelor member who is struggling to find a sustaining and enabling proclamation in the liturgy. The age question might be best dealt with by combining the understandings of the parents involved with some guidelines worked out carefully by the congregation or representative committees or task groups.

The depth of conversation required to arrive at guidelines for children at worship is more evidence of how basic worship is to the total church and how reflective it is of the church's life. Unless this concern is detached from its context and is handled in a surface manner, it will bring forth some very fundamental considerations. How much maturity is required to participate in a Christian service of worship? The "problem" of children at worship might indicate that we are too verbal or too intellectually oriented. Children are entitled to be heard as well as seen at worship. The church decides how a service for all the members best expresses this.

Do Women Know Their Place?

Some denominations have almost completely, if not totally, eliminated any legislation that would prevent a woman from serving any office or performing any church role. Others have taken measurable steps in this direction. The election of a female president of the National Council of Churches in the U.S.A. in 1970 symbolized some of these gains. Some local churches have women pastors, and a few United Methodist bishops have appointed women to their cabinets. Despite these examples, however, we are a long way from complete recognition of women as full human beings in the church. Each church's service of worship illustrates how equally or unequally women are accepted.

In some congregations, of course, the absence of women in worship leadership tells us little more than that neither laymen nor laywomen are asked to lead and possibly do not seek to lead. Women have always had a very strong role in the life of local congregations. The basic strength of local churches is in the women, but too often they have been given their own organizations in which they can provide leadership and from which they can send "representatives" to the governing body or bodies of the church. The service of worship presents the story quite well, ordinarily, with women representing the majority in the pews and yet being almost excluded from the altar area.

If a woman or women were included in the usher corps, read the Scriptures occasionally, assisted in the distribution of the elements at Holy Communion, and even said a few words from the pulpit, most worshipers might gather that the job of board chairman, lay leader, and other leadership positions were open or might soon be open to females as well as males. Our liturgy helps us see how seriously we believe that in Christ there is neither male nor female.

Do We Have to Talk About Money?

Few acts of worship reflect the people's understanding of life as well as those which involve money. To some the offering plates are necessary evils. A very sensitive lady once offered to raise equivalent funds if I would eliminate the offering of money which "spoiled an otherwise beautiful Easter service." A pastor who hears this kind of plea does well to recognize that this request is less of a liturgical consideration than it is an indication of a basic confusion about the sacred and the secular or the spiritual and the material. Services of worship offer a good tip-off on the degree to which we regard that which is material as evil, compared with the extent to which we really accept the incarnation—the Word made flesh.

A liturgy study on the appropriateness of a money offering in worship will also explore much deeper areas if the subject is treated comprehensively. Embarrassment about interrupting sacred time with things of this world points to a dualism that works against fulfillment in our relationships with other persons and with the world about us. Certain activities are often considered spiritual—singing hymns, praying, reading the Bible, and receiving Holy Communion. But "taking up money" is in another category. A money offering is considered by some to be justified only because its results will enable us to do the spiritual exercises just mentioned.

The church's doctrine of the incarnation tells us that we

find God in this world of persons and things. The kingdom of God is in the midst of us. If our services of worship keep themselves relatively clean of the material world by acting apologetically about offerings of money, they indicate their rejection of a belief in the incarnation.

The other side of the coin is the centering of attention on money and statistical successes as worship's primary goal. A friend says that she still recalls the disappointment that she and her husband suffered when they attended church immediately following his tour of combat duty in World War II. The total "service" that morning was a money-raising session for one of that congregation's favorite causes.

The giving of our money as an act of worship can be a prime opportunity for the people to dramatize the giving of themselves. As an economy-oriented society we attach considerable significance to financial contributions. Our money represents our willingness to identify with, to support, and to maintain the church in its ministry and proclamation of the Good News. Rather than hurrying by it, we would do well to call greater attention to our act. One step is to eliminate euphemisms and proclaim that we will worship by giving our *money*. Another step is to make it clear that this is not only a worshipful act. The church needs the actual money it receives in order to carry out its ministry—to buy floor wax, pay utilities, provide salaries, and all those other earthly things.

Some congregations are now bringing their money forward to the altar-table. They are finding the trip forward with the money to be an added opportunity to express their willingness or even eagerness to offer themselves. Even if one's pledge is paid through the mail, the moving of people forward with "loose change" is a strong reminder that we are called not only to hear and speak but also to actively enter into the healing ministry of God.

Evangelism—for All

Evangelism is the proclaiming of the Good News. It must be proclaimed new and heard new by every creature in each new experience of his life. The service of worship will express whether we understand evangelism in such a way or whether we use it as a strategy for institutional gain.

The church proclaims what has been proclaimed to it through the event of Jesus Christ if it is truly evangelistic. The Word is that anyone who trusts God, who will commit himself to that understanding, that life-style, that new creation made known in Christ, most certainly will know that God will transcend all defeats with victory. He does not prevent them or do away with them, but gives victory in the midst of them. This is the message of the cross. This is evangelism.

It is a call for those outside the church. What do we say about our own convictions and experience if those of us in the church are not eager to witness to others? If the gospel really does identify the transforming power in my life, then surely I will not be content to keep it to myself. What a contradiction that would be!

Evangelism is no less a call to church members than it is for persons most distant from its doors—in mileage or in identification. The professional evangelistic visitor for a large church told me once that he recognized that those of us in that church were not perfect, but isn't it wonderful, he said, that we aren't bank robbers and murderers like some outside our walls. To appeal to prospective members to come join the good people misses evangelism as far as does the appeal to "say the magic words and become entitled to heaven when you die." Evangelism is a call to those inside the church who pray thus, "I thank thee, God, that I am not like other men."

Rather than approach services of worship as "occasions for evangelism," we need to understand that genuine Christian worship will make clear that evangelism is what the faith is all about. Evangelism certainly can include the recruitment of members, but this effort is only a part of the total evangelistic thrust. The term "evangelism" is really another name for what is meant by the "calling" of the church; another term which defines it is "mission."

The World as Our Parish

Christian worship sends us out with assurance that God's blessing will be with us in our commitment to mission in the world. That is, if our service of worship is effectively Christian, the weekday life of our congregation will be mission-oriented. A congregation that is impatient with injustice, is quick to feed the hungry, and visits those who are sick and in prison will find these concerns reflected in its worship and in turn will find its courage in commitment renewed.

Liturgy has many ways of both reflecting our concern about others and of pushing us toward more participation in God's healing activity. Not only do we include the hungry in our prayers, but we can also add to this a container in the sanctuary to receive food offerings. We call attention to those who are ill, and members know that this calls for a note, a visit, or a telephone call. A section of the liturgy which includes a story of tragic injustice to a blind Negro teenager in a penal institution can bring immediate action to see that the conditions that brought the tragedy about are corrected before others suffer.

The church can lend its voice to various claims through announcements at the close of the service, urging voter registration, seeking volunteers for tutoring, enlisting help in transporting a child to a clinic each day, suggesting letters to congressmen and others concerning pending legislation. These suggestions comprise only a small part of Sunday morning's worship, but their presence is quite vital.

The presence of certain persons in the service can, by their color or other identification, say that this church is involving itself beyond its own walls. We know the danger of thinking that a racial problem is solved if one or two members of another race are present. This is not what I am suggesting. It is likely, however, that a congregation deeply involved in community life beyond its own immediate radius will begin to have services of worship which include more than members of just one social, economic, or educational group.

Part II

The Content and Communication of Worship

4

The Life We Proclaim

The first requirement for Christian worship is that it be radically faithful to the gospel of Jesus Christ. Christians have been called to proclaim the Word that every human being is offered joy, fullness, meaning, and healing in every occasion of his life.

These are extravagant words to those outside the Christian faith; for Christians themselves the words can become dulled and be spoken glibly. Therefore, the second requirement for Christian worship is that its urgent message to all people must be communicated in such a way that man-made stumbling blocks to faith are removed and the Word comes through, judging and comforting. It is by these two criteria that today's services of worship should be tested.

Content and form, although not identical, are certainly intimately related. If the medium is not the message, nevertheless the medium through which the faith is communicated is of indispensable importance in creating the sense of reality in worship. For example, the forms through which the congregation expresses its praise, and the liveliness with which this is done, may well convey the sense of praise more effectively than the words used. But admitting the important interrelationship between content and communication, we must now ask, first, what is the content of Christian worship?

Worship Is God-Centered

"God-centered" is a highly dangerous phrase. In a day of growing suspicion of religious language, the seeking person who is attempting to be intellectually honest is often frightened by this phrase. It appears to point away from man and his problems and points up or out to what seems to function as a cipher. It is also dangerous to the smug who feel that they are God-centered because they have repelled the storming of the doors by people carrying banners, playing guitars, and singing "They Will Know We Are Christians by Our Love." But neither is a service of worship necessarily God-centered because we use King James language, keep the children from talking or running about in God's house, schedule the service at the proper hour on Sunday, or put a cross on the top of the building.

We center our worship on God when we acknowledge that God is surely in our place of worship, but that he is no less present in every other place. God is at the center of worship when we are faithful to the scriptural proclamation of who God is and how he is at work in our world and in our lives. It is not those services which simply say, "Lord, Lord," but those services of worship whose content makes the Father known to us that are not far from the kingdom of God. A service of worship makes the Father known to us if it calls us to acknowledge the Holy.

The Holy comes into the experiences of everyone. We are not speaking of religious music, books, prayers, or of any other creation when we speak of that which is holy. The Holy meets and envelops each of us time and again in our daily experiences. We will say more about the meaning of this meeting and enveloping later. An important function of the liturgy is to make this experience of meeting God explicit in form and symbol. We are called to celebrate the constant presence of God, who by his grace is most certainly present at the time of worship but is no less present in all those other moments of our lives.

God-centered worship is not an attempt to create a "religious experience." What I have generally been referring to as "worship" in this book is really the *rite of worship*, not necessarily the experience. When we speak of our moment-to-moment worship of God in spirit and in truth— our daily encounters with his presence and our faithful response—we are pointing to those experiences that are *not* directed by our own planning. The service of worship which comes at times and places which *we* designate is the rite or celebration. We cannot afford to look upon the service of worship, the Sunday morning ritual, as a time to attempt the creation of the experience of the Holy, for such is not a possibility. The ritual may or may not be a meaningful, God-filled experience for us. We may hope this will be the case, but *every* occasion of life holds the potential. We cannot say, "Lo here," or, "Lo there." God's meeting us is not subject to man's whims or even his most careful thought and planning.

God is going to meet us whether we ever go to church or not. And we will sometimes respond in faith to these meetings, and in unfaith at other times. Services of worship enable us to look back at our lives and try to understand how the Holy was with us and to consider our response. We are also enabled to look ahead and consider what our future encounters with God will mean. The service of worship is celebration in the true sense of the word.

Celebration is sometimes used to mean "happy times." In the language of the church, celebration is the "making public," the "pointing to." This may be the happy occasions of weddings and Easter or the sad times of funerals and Good Friday. Christian celebration is not the attempt to make happy noises on tragic or bitter occasions. It will indeed take full cognizance of sadness and desolation, but its concern is to bring such experiences out into the open in the light of the transcendent One who brings life even in death. We celebrate all of life. We publish it, we hold it up. This we do that we may proclaim that God redeems it all, not that he makes it go away or makes us feel good about it.

The validity of "happenings" within the church is certainly not being challenged. Dismissing them out of hand, which is their usual form of dismissal, is too hasty. Most such movements are signals of gaps or deficiencies in our congregational life. Those who reject them might do well to first understand why they have come into being and what message they might have for us. Happenings, however, are not substitutes for the Christian drama of worship into which we are called.

Our hour of worship never exists for its own sake. That would be to lose its life. Although we would probably stop going to church if we *never* experienced God's presence in the worship hours, nevertheless, we are not looking for a "religious experience" to justify our rite. When during the service of worship we experience genuine confession, true adoration and praise, or a deep awareness of a commitment, we are grateful. Validation of the service, however, is not contingent on whether this transitory and fleeting experience comes. Our worship always proclaims that ultimate reality before whom all beings live, Christians and non-Christians, the faithful and the unfaithful.

True worship is always ready to interrupt itself in the middle of a prayer to offer help to the needy neighbor. Although participation in common worship and in the public proclamation of the Christian faith, some may say, is the first demand on the man of faith, at the same time it is the first activity that must be set aside the very moment faith makes its claim—when the neighbor's need calls. Our services of worship become religion-centered, not God-centered, when they look primarily to their own devices to create an immediate sense of God's presence. Worship is truly God-centered when it enables the worshiper to identify the presence of the Holy in each daily experience and when it points us to the shape which our faithful response should take. Liturgy is indeed concerned with what the worshiper experiences *during* the service, but of much greater importance is the concern that worship witness *beyond* itself to the whole of life.

What Do We Say About the Holy?

Christians are not content simply to say that in worship we come into the presence of the Holy. The gospel has a definite understanding of what such a declaration is about. Modern-day disciples cannot hide behind the words, "God is totally other than man; he is infinite and man is finite. Man, therefore, can say nothing about God for he is attempting to use finite language to speak of that which is infinite." This statement sounds humble enough and certainly reflects a problem; yet it denies its own claim, for it has already made a very definite assertion about God. We *will* talk of God. The question is, how shall we do it? Even if a national poll reports that 98 percent of the people believe in "God," this report tells us little more than that 98 percent of the population said "yes" to the question. We can only guess at what they meant by their answers.

Christian worship makes no offer to explain away the mystery of life. The mystery is revealed to us, not solved for us. The mystery to which our faith points is not in the category of "knowledge not yet discovered by man." When we speak of man unraveling the mysteries of the world, we are speaking of a different realm. Technology will apparently enable us to continue making amazing and wonderful discoveries about our earth and about space. Behavioral scientists will continue to discover more about our inner workings. But these discoveries are only a process that goes on *within* the mystery of being. The scientist or man in space does not have, by reason of his technical information, more clarity about God than a tomato farmer in east Texas.

A great function of our intellect is its informing us that we cannot totally comprehend reality or even come close. The Christian church has done poorly when it has attempted to define the nature of God as an entity. This kind of approach is usually behind the "Do you believe in God?" kind of question. Christian worship focuses primarily on *how* God is at work in the world and leaves the intellectual games to others. The very definition of God in the Christian faith removes the belief in God from a matter of mental assent. Our liturgy holds up the activities of God that are such a vital part of every man's existence, names them as God's work, and invites man to respond to them in faith.

Our Response to God's Presence

"Comforting the afflicted and afflicting the comfortable" is an old phrase that sets forth the activity of God. We never respond with consistency or with unmixed emotions to God's activity in our lives. We fear the Holy and yet are fascinated by it. It both repels us and attracts us. When our service of worship makes clear the presence of God, we want to hide, to undo him, to discredit and rid ourselves of him. This will be our response if it is truly God to whom the liturgy has pointed, but just as surely there is the other necessary response. We are also drawn to him, we want to commit ourselves to him without reservation. The act of worship must hold before us both these experiences if it truly publishes the Word.

Biblical images remind us that God's ways are not our ways and his thoughts are not our thoughts. They tell us also, however, that the Word became flesh. The distance that separates man from God can never be bridged, yet we are reminded that God is in the midst of us. He knows our thoughts before we know them; he is never far away. These two understandings of God are inseparable. Man is enabled by Christian liturgy to recognize that God will always be present to him in ways that bring both these responses. Even if he does not experience both these responses, or even one of them, in the ritual, he participates in the more significant and permanent role of having heard this truth again and is able to proclaim it.

Out of History

Naming names is another way of being specific about the God we worship. We are a historical people. We didn't just think up this faith. Our celebration joins with a great host of past witnesses. We remember our many fathers in the faith of whom we are a part. When someone asks, "What do you mean about obedience to God?" we start the reels turning and present the Abraham-Isaac sacrifice story. Rather than offer a theological treatise, we might answer a question about the wonderful and terrifying meaning of God's gift of freedom by recounting the Exodus. And we look to the New Testament and exhibit the testimony of all those who had their lives made new through Jesus of Nazareth, his crucifixion and resurrection.

The service of Holy Communion is the greatest example of this kind of grounding in history. What better example can we have of the action of God in allowing man his freedom to destroy as well as to bring healing? What more powerful symbol can show how we use our freedom as an "occasion of the flesh" by killing the One who brings life and still have God redeem it all by offering victory and light in the midst of the worst kind of defeat and darkness? Our worship identifies God by his activities.

"If you tell me that a friend loves me, I can understand that, but if you tell me that God loves me, it means nothing. What do I care about a supernatural being out there somewhere loving me?" Liturgy answers these questions by pointing to the meaning of God's love in the life of the worshiper —how it makes its impact. Our worship is a dramatizing of how God shows his love to us and how existence is changed by this love. That is the drama of Holy Communion, of Christmas, of Easter, and of all our worship. Worship holds before us the constant activity by which God transcends each experience of our lives. It demonstrates that in all things God works for good with those who respond to his gift.

In Christian worship God is not presented as a love-struck entity, a warm glob of emotion in which I can take comfort when the people about me have rejected me. He is the One who shows he loves me by what he is always doing for me. Even when his action appears to be against me, he is nevertheless bringing me new life. The people of Israel did not decide they needed a Jesus Christ. Through its various literary forms, the New Testament tells of this breaking through of salvation in a carpenter as the loving action of God. God so loves this world that he *acts*. Even while we are yet sinners, he acts. Even though we continue to reject him, he continues to act. And his act is love. Worship which makes this love evident is God-centered worship.

A Word for All—Now

A total inclusiveness is also demanded by our first test of worship. If the content of liturgy is soundly Christian, the congregation will know that the Word it hears and proclaims is for *all* men. The one who is enslaved by injustice stands in need of the same Word as the man who enslaves him. If the message we proclaim is not the same message for Negroes, Mexican-Americans, and American Indians as it is for Caucasians, then it is not the gospel of Jesus Christ. It is the same evangel for the poor as it is for the rich, for the young as for the old. Certainly it must be channeled and dramatized in those peculiar ways that make its meaning clear, but we have only one gospel; we need only one gospel. To speak otherwise is to deny our faith.

One man objects, "It is well for you middle-class and affluent people to emphasize *this* world, to tell us not to live in the world of tomorrow, for you have the goods of this life. You have food, clothing, education, and a place in the mainstream of society. But my people do not have this. We cannot look at the present life as you do because all of these comforts and benefits lie ahead for us. We must have a theology of hope that looks beyond today to a better life here or in a world to come." Christian worship which reveals God in Christ will make it clear that genuine life fulfillment is not conditioned by color, status, age, economic condition, or any other barrier. Only man's unwillingness to receive life *where he is* can separate him from the loving action of God. Our liturgy points this out to us by holding before us the cross.

Surely we cannot ignore our brother's statement to us. We miss the whole point of the Christian faith if we do not recognize injustices and if we do not act to correct them. We must work on behalf of our neighbor that he may have the benefits of our society. We also fail him, however, if we pretend that the reception of life and the possibility for celebrating and knowing the joy of living is determined only by improving living conditions. God's gift of life cannot be defeated by conditions.

Worship looks to the past without embarrassment. We have recalled our historic "name-dropping" and our past events. We are our past. We can recognize each other and talk about ourselves with meaning only when we remember our previous days and years. We are concerned also about the future, for our future is even now a part of our lives. I assume I will have a tomorrow and I assume that it will have a certain shape, even though my whole past life has told me that almost limitless world events, health, weather, and some seemingly trivial happenings can make its shape radically different from my expectations. Death may come and I won't even be around to experience tomorrow. But the anticipation of a certain kind of future is a part of my present moment. My immediate identity consists not only of who I have been and who I might have been, but also of who I might be in the future. Christian worship celebrates the total range of living; it celebrates the past ("For all the saints, who from their labors rest"), prays for the present ("Grant us courage for the facing of this hour"), and hopes for the future ("Come, thou long-expected Jesus").

Good News—Life Is *Here!*

Test the content of worship to see if it is really the Good News. We don't ask if it is *some* good news. We ask if it is *the* Good News, if it is the proclamation that gives one the assurance that his life counts ultimately, that he is loved and is cared for far more than he could ever care for himself. Does it tell him that, although he will die, there is One who makes sense out of his life, receives it, and ever holds it as a part of all that has been, is, and ever will be? He does not need to put his hope in a world that will come to him after his death; he is affirmed now.

We often think of those who refute "modern" thinking

and hold fast to a concept of reward (heaven) and punishment (hell) as being the fundamentalists. "Fundamentalism" seldom means sticking with the fundamentals of the faith. When death comes we hear, "He has gone to be with God." Christian liturgy offers the Good News by saying that we don't have to wait to be with God. *This* is my Father's world. Christian liturgy must remind us that God is not pushed out of this world and is out waiting for us to join him when we die. Christian worship makes clear his invitation to join him now, in this life.

God so loved the world . . . . Too often the faith has indicated that God doesn't love this world. He just couldn't make it *his* world, apparently, and since he is not powerful enough to enter into this world, he asks us to stick it out and hope for an early death ("On Jordan's stormy banks I stand and cast a wistful eye"). We can then join him in his world—which is heaven. When worship is faithful to the Christian faith, it will make it clear that we need not escape this world to find God. Eternal life need not wait for our death; it occurs when we respond in faith to God's claim on us.

Worship as Revelation

Another content claim on authentic Christian worship calls for our liturgy to be revelation rather than propaganda. Paul Tillich says that "modern art is not propaganda but revelation. It shows that the reality of our existence is as it is." [1] Our worship betrays God when it attempts to present the world in reductionist terms rather than in the way the world really is. Art in our churches has too often been propaganda. It has attempted to identify the "holy" with

[1] Paul Tillich, *The Courage to Be* (New Haven: Yale University Press, 1952), p. 147.

71

particular objects, to squeeze life into a religious mold. The music of worship has not reflected the world of tension, passion, and conflict in which we live. As with its treatment of art the church has used music to set forth a simplified and thus distorted view of life. True Christian worship accepts the whole world as God's and has no need to reduce any of its expressions to propaganda.

5

The Drama of Reality

Worship is drama. Many laymen and pastors alike know that liturgy is usually considered to consist of three acts—confession, praise, and offering—although modified versions are plentiful and may have their own worth. Certainly we shall work to find the best forms, but what is of chief importance is that we understand how this drama relates to us and how we relate to the drama.

Does it seem offensive to refer to worship as drama, as playacting? If so, it could be that we evaluate our time in worship as signifying something other than it really is and as less than it is called to be. Drama is not "true," it is "true to," which gives the form peculiar relevance to the concerns of faith. To think of worship as drama could well remind us that we can't command God to be on hand when we beckon. Recognition of worship as drama could well punch away at our puffed-up ideas of ourselves and what we can create.

Offense at this terminology might also help to make us aware that worship is much more than our presentation of it. To consider that services of worship are *the* meeting with God, and not the occasion of dramatizing, infers that he meets us only once a week under certain circumstances, and only then when we name him. With the image of drama we point beyond the walls of the church and beyond the hour of worship to his limitless presence.

The drama which relates to us and to which we relate is not considered simply "one of the best." Christians are bold enough to call it *the* drama. We do not say that this is what your life is about if you are a Christian. We say, *"This is what life is about."* Worship knowingly speaks from the faith of creatures called Christians, but it dares speak on behalf of all. The reality is not playacting. The reality is life itself.

How can limited and finite creatures be so absurd as to say what is the truth about life? We say that the gospel is the truth regardless of our own failures to receive it as such. The sum of two and two is four, even if we are told this by someone who always adds it up to be five.

We bet our lives that the gospel we proclaim is *the* truth. We enter into the total act of worship knowing that we are not absolute in our knowledge, power, or love. We know it and everyone else knows it. We also know that our lives have been made whole when we have committed them to this One to whom we point. We, therefore, put aside all the "we think," "in our view," "others may differ," kind of talk and say without embarrassment, "Thus saith the Lord."

Would you accuse Paul Muni of being a hypocrite by pretending to be Louis Pasteur in a movie? Was Raymond Burr hypocritical to assume the role of an attorney on television when he, in fact, has never gone to law school? Ridiculous, but no more ridiculous than the charge of hypocrisy against those who come each week to assume the role of how a person of faith lives when he is confronted each moment by Almighty God. We rehearse the drama. We enter into it. We may not be experiencing confession during the prayer of confession. This existential confession might come "out of turn" during the offering of our money, or it might not come at all. We act out, however, what confession "looks like" when it is consistent with New Testament faith.

Can we afford to say prayers of confession or prayers of offering when we don't really feel that way? We not only

74

say "yes," this is possible, but that to do so is essential to our faith. A Christian is called to act in love whether he has a warm feeling toward his neighbor or not. He is not hypocritical within the Christian understanding because he lends a hand to someone he resents or dislikes. As an honest man he knows that he does not have equally warm feelings toward all people. He has negative feelings also. Christian love certainly encompasses all forms of love—friendship, love between man and woman, love of family and friends, love of country, etc. Christian love, however, is not dependent on likes or dislikes. Our gospel tells us that we are to show the love of God to our neighbor whether we feel it or not. The same is true of the claim in worship. We take on the role of one who confesses, one who praises, and one who offers himself without reservation, not only when we feel like it, but on each occasion. How truly then does worship reflect life!

Earlier I said that confession for Christians is not an act but a stance of life by which we meet each moment. Viewing ourselves as actors who set forth the meaning of confession each Sunday morning underlines this position. We cannot afford to "wait for the spirit to move us." This weekly dramatizing does not guarantee that if we go through these Christian services regularly, we shall begin to take on these characteristics. Regular practice of the rite of faithfulness does not automatically make people become more faithful human beings. We continue to forget who we are called to be. All men ask themselves, "Why did I do that foolish thing? I know better than that. Why do I keep forgetting?" It is because we do keep forgetting that we participate regularly in this drama. We cannot do without such constant reminder. Worship keeps reminding us of what faith "looks like" in our corporate and personal lives. Even if the order of service bulletin appears the same from week to week, yet the weekly drama comes at us somewhat differently on each occasion. God uses the liturgy as he uses all creation in an endless variety of ways to bring us a fresh revelation of himself.

If we tried to construct a service of worship each Sunday that would match the moods of people or match their "felt worship needs," we should be doomed to failure. Some people's moods will change between the time they park their car and the beginning of the first hymn. This is as risky as trying to provide a mood for people to take with them. A man who leaves a service with a religious glow could lose it all if he found his car fender scratched. We are not really in the mood-and-feeling business. The liturgy provides us with a model of God's gift and the Christian response by which we can determine the way in which we will meet the future—including much more serious matters than scratched fenders.

The whole gospel is presented, though in fragments, each Sunday. It comes to those who approach the drama with a feeling of hostility, to those with strong feelings of love, to those who are at peace with the world, to those who are anxious, and to persons in any other emotional or mental state. It says to all, "Let's take it from the top!" We begin the action with a rehearsal of our past through the act of confession, move into our present with praise and proclamation, and finally offer our future to the God of all life.

What We Bring to the Drama

Our emphasis has been on the "objective reality" of the Christian liturgy—the historical proclamation of God's revelation of life through Christ. The reminder is always coming through, however, that how we are involved in this drama

is an essential part of it. To the Christian rites that dramatize life we bring ourselves—our feelings as well as our in-
tellects. We cannot afford not to bring our total selves.

The problem of feelings and worship was pointed up for
me through a family's absence from worship for a period
of time following the funeral services for their daughter.
Two or three weeks' absence from worship is not unusual
for some persons, of course, but this situation took on signs
of a more permanent nature. They had no plans to come
back. The mother said that she was afraid to go back into
the sanctuary of the church for fear that she would burst
into tears. Neither the funeral service nor their past church
years had enabled the family to know that the very place to
bring sad feelings is the church. Of course, some people
know this. They come to church the very next Sunday after
a funeral, thinking, "Suppose I do start crying right in the
middle of this service. If it isn't OK for me to cry in church,
what's wrong with me and the church?" We bring tears to
the church, and we certainly might expect a few laughs.

Worship Can Be Fun

What a shame that pastors have caused laymen to be
nervous about the phrase, "I enjoyed your sermon." If some
layman is unable to keep his enthusiasm in check and blurts
out these words, he usually asks quickly, "But I'm not supposed to enjoy it, am I?" We were well meaning
to point up that sermons are not intended primarily as
entertainment and that the sermon that is least enjoyed
might well be the most appropriate one. What a dismal
idea, however, to think that sermons should not be enjoyed!

A music director friend of mine made a great response to
an inquiring choir member who asked about the validity
of a scheduled "Swingle Singers" type anthem (no words,

just do-be-do-be-do-be sounds). The anthem texts each Sunday were usually rather profound and theologically significant, the director admitted, but he had decided to do this one just because it was fun. Fun is not out of place in worship. Worship welcomes the whole person, and this most certainly includes his feelings.

Two "Stages" in Worship

We do best to talk about the rationale of worship before a service and after it, but not during the celebration itself. Rather than provide explanatory notes of what we are doing and why, we make the service stronger by simply going about our business of worship. An exception to this suggestion, however, could be an occasional service, Sunday morning or at another time, when we further analyze the form and content of our service of worship and reflect on its relationship to our personal lives.

At this occasional service two "stages" would be set. One stage is the scene of the pulpit and altar-table. The other stage is occupied by a narrator standing at the side, but in view of the people. The service begins with a statement from the narrator telling what is about to happen. He explains that his role will be to introduce each section of the service of worship which is about to begin. He will stop the service between acts to comment on the meaning of what has happened or of what is to follow, or both. For example, the narrator might say immediately following the sermon, "We have been involved in praise and in a witness to God's Word. As Christians we respond to what we have said with our mouths by our commitment to action. Let us put our lives in God's hands and dare to do his will in the world about us." In this service the scene will constantly switch between the congregation at worship and their pausing to listen to the narrator interpreting their acts. When the entire service is over, the congregation may be given the opportunity to raise further questions or offer their response to what has taken place.

A variation of this type of educational presentation which requires more work could serve as an addition to the above service, if not in place of it. A small drama group acting out life situations replaces the narrator after he explains what is about to take place. The focus then moves back and forth from the liturgical event to an enactment of an event in our daily lives which corresponds. Here is an example.

Following an opening hymn, the liturgy begins with "Words of Judgment" from the Scripture. The sentences are read and the scene shifts to the drama group. They portray how these words come to us in common experiences. A man and his son are sitting in front of television, watching an exciting football game. The telephone rings and the son moves to answer it. "Who would call at a crucial time like this? If that's for me, say that I'm not in," the father tells him. The boy does this and then asks, "Daddy, why is it wrong for me not to tell the truth when you ask me where I have been and yet it isn't wrong for me to tell people you aren't here?"

The subject might be of a more serious nature, depicting a man being told that his unwillingness to yield a right-of-way has resulted in death for another driver. Whatever the situation, the drama group makes it clear that God's judgment comes to us in *our* world.

What happens when we receive God's judgment? If we do not respond in faith, we can offer excuses and rationalizations. But if we respond Christianly, we confess our sin. The scene moves to the liturgy and the congregation enters into a prayer of confession. Back now to the drama group to see how confession appears when it takes on concrete expression in living. The father is confessing to his son through whom God's judgment has come or the driver is making his response to the news of a death caused by his insistence on being right.

The dramatic skits can follow one story line or they can each stand alone. Staging can be rather extensive or quite simple. Modifications include placards brought in and placed before the congregation prior to each liturgical act. When we start describing this possibility of informing the congregation about worship, so many possibilities appear that our problem really becomes a matter of choosing between alternatives. Whatever the format, and whether it is presented on Sunday morning, at a congregational business meeting, or elsewhere, the congregation will have a deeper look into the relationship of liturgy to everyday life.

A Message to Would-Be Actors

Finally, the theater offers us some important help. One director says that the basic question an honest actor should ask before accepting a specific role is: "Can I give myself fully to this role?" Such a question can only be answered after posing other questions, such as, "Does this role set forth a believable person caught up in believable relationships?" "Am I convinced that I can take on such a role with integrity?" "Do I want to enter into the creation of such a role?" If these questions can be answered yes, that is a clear indication that the actor will be able to commit himself to his part in the total drama. It is evident that the question is not whether or not I will take off my clothes on stage or whether or not I will say certain words.

Once accepting the role, the actor is prepared to do whatever would be true to that character caught up in the relationships in which he is presented. What is involved here is not some self-induced form of schizophrenia; the actor remains who he is but voluntarily explores the depths and heights of the character. His own creative intellect is always present but remains in the background, quietly evaluating the authenticity of each response. The commitment is a deep one, including the emotions and the intellect. As far as it is humanly possible, the whole person must be involved.

Our role in the drama of worship is quite similar. When we elect to be present as part of the congregation, we have made a commitment. We come recklessly to assume the role of Christians. Are we not, in fact, called to be Christ's body? We must ask, therefore, is this role a believable one to which we can give ourselves fully now and in this world? Can we honestly say that the Christian faith is a possibility today? With some idea of what is involved, do I really want to take on such a role? Will I be able to act as it calls me to act, to be true to my role as it relates to the rest of the body? Am I ready to accept crucifixion? Am I ready to live my life cast in such a role? To be present in the service of worship is to say "yes" to these soul-searching questions.

6

Proclaiming Life in Confession, Praise, and Offering

The major sections or acts of worship—confession, praise, and offering—within the service provide a helpful way of examining the Christian content of our liturgy. The following pages look at the content of the gospel by approaching the faith through these specific areas.

Confession—Telling Our Name

The true meaning of Christian confession is not simply a matter of opinion. We look to our biblical heritage—to the Old Testament as well as to the New—to determine what it means to confess Christianly. We look also to our church fathers as they have interpreted Scriptures through these many years. One of the most lively stories to help identify what it means to confess to Almighty God is the story of Jacob and his wrestling. In the Old Testament names had significance. Knowing the events surrounding Jacob's birth, his trickery to get Esau's birthright, and his deception in obtaining his father's blessings, we aren't surprised to find that his name refers to his character—the one who trips up by the heel. The demand, therefore, that Jacob tell his name is God's demand that he admit his life. He wasn't asked to tell the evil things he had done. He wasn't asked to say that he was sorry. When he said that his name was Jacob, God blessed him and changed his name to Israel. To say it another way, when he confessed his life before God, God forgave him and raised him up a new person.

The service of confession has been treated shabbily by

free churches in the past generation. Not having dealt with confession biblically, as the Jacob story presented it, the church classified the act as one of recounting our evil deeds or of generally saying that we were bad. How could a generation of persons who had the whole world moving on to bigger and better things dare include a section in its worship which spoke badly of man? If every day and in every way we were getting better and better, we certainly could not retain such negative positions in our worship. Positive thinkers don't want to work with negative material. In this context we can acknowledge that we aren't perfect. We can take the bite out of that, however, by asking, "But who is?"

Our nation indicated how it misunderstood confession with its response to President John F. Kennedy's death. The city fathers of Dallas worked overtime to make it clear that this tragedy was not the fault of the citizens of that city and should in no way reflect on the city's character. They were embarrassed with the attempts of some local ministers who tried to make a statement of confession on behalf of themselves. A number of citizens threatened the life of one pastor who made a confessional statement on television. One member wrote, "Our pastor told us that we too had to share in the death of the President but the Warren Commission report proved that he was wrong. Only one man was to blame."

Dallasites could not comprehend what it meant to confess, thinking this meant that we all participated in the plot and that we are thereby worse than citizens of other cities. Other cities in our nation shared this ignorance of confession by regarding residents of Dallas to be in need of confession, since they were, in fact, more sinful than themselves. The Isaiah model for confession in an occasion such as this is appropriate throughout the world—"I am a man of unclean lips and I dwell in the midst of a people of unclean lips." A more contemporary model is that of the churchmen in Germany following World War II. The very persons who had most strongly resisted Hitler were the ones who brought forth a heart-searching statement of confession for the nation.

What and Why We Confess

A probing into the meaning of sin must come prior to a Christian expression of confession. A biblical understanding of sin differs drastically from that popular secular understanding which believes that sin is simply breaking the rules. It is "wrongdoing" with an assumption that all know what that means. Biblically, however, sin is much more basic. Sin is a state or condition of man in which he separates himself from God, neighbor, and from himself. It is man's efforts to deny his creatureliness, to claim for himself the role of God. This stance separates him from life and expresses itself through concrete acts which destroy and fracture those about him as well as destroying himself. A sick tree puts forth sick fruit. Man's sin, therefore, is not that he is a creature. His sin is his attempt to pretend that he is all-wise, all-powerful, and all-good. Christian worship makes this condition of man known and points to the "sins," symptoms, or manifestations of this state of separation.

Our confession is really Good News. Only when we start from our true condition is there hope of our being made new. God's judgment on us is always at the same time his love. He judges us to redeem us. We are free to live the authentic life only when we can acknowledge that our present life is one of pretense. God's word to us that we are sinners is meant to raise us out of that phony and death-dealing existence in which we attempt to escape from him. Confession in genuine Christian liturgy announces that creatureliness is not a second-rate kind of life. Genesis tells us that God looked upon his total creation, including man, and said that it was good. We are called to live as creatures, to rejoice in this life. Creatureliness is not a consolation prize. It signifies potentiality and power and joy in achievement.

Christian worship speaks of forgiveness as healing, not just as a legalistic act by which marks are removed from the negative side of our ledger. We have no question about being forgiven if the liturgy truly expresses the New Testament faith. "If we confess our sin, God is faithful and just and will forgive us our sin and cleanse us from all unrighteousness." This, again, is God's love. His love is always present, bringing healing. The recognition of who we are and of *who we are called to be* makes it possible for us to raise our heads and throw ourselves into the ministry of love. "He breaks the power of canceled sin, he sets the prisoner free."

A failure to accept our forgiveness is evidence that we do not really understand what confession is. A style of life which requires my carrying my past sin on my back or an armload of guilt is not the new life to which Christians are called. To remain in guilt is to exist in death. God calls us to life. The man who accepts his gift of forgiveness is free to live a life of praise.

For What Are We Thankful?

"It is very meet and right that we should at all times give thanks to God." So says our Holy Communion liturgy, but if we listen to most extemporaneous prayers we find that we thank God only for the good things of life—health, peace, prosperity, friends, and sunshine. Surely a Christian recognizes the value of all these expressions of the good life.

He wants them for himself and for others and is not embarrassed by this desire. Our service of praise rightly includes these gifts. But who wouldn't be grateful for such blessings? The Christian, who keeps looking up at that cross over his head, knows that worship must make clear that we are grateful for much more than those gifts which we call "good."

A man in a hospital made this witness to his pastor. He and his family had suffered minor injuries in an accident which totally demolished his car. The pastor told him that he was sure that he must feel grateful to God for the fact that all had survived in such remarkable condition. The man agreed that he was grateful to God. He asked, however, if it would be possible to praise God if his whole family had been killed and he had been critically hurt.

Christian praise is not contingent on our circumstances. One Sunday morning the pastor of a rather affluent congregation urged his people to count their blessings. "Some of you think that you have little to be thankful for," he reminded them, "but remember that you have sufficient clothes, adequate health, and enough transportation to make it possible for you to be present in this service." Perhaps this was quite appropriate. We do take our possessions for granted, thinking we have so little when such is not the case. Such a reminder and such thankfulness are certainly not anti-Christian. Yet Christian praise is of another dimension. We praise the One who gives life and meaning when we are deprived of everything the preacher can think of.

Picture the most desolate and hopeless contemporary condition you can imagine. Now say that the person in this deplorable situation, if he is a man of faith, can praise God. If he can't, then his God is not the One whom the cross proclaims. Only when we can also give thanks to God in illness, war, storm, strife, hunger, and even in death can our praise for the "goods" of life be genuinely Christian. This is foolishness to some. Are we to say in our liturgy that we have no preference as between sickness and health, war and peace, hunger and plenty? We are saying no such thing. We are most seriously concerned about all these. The Lord knows we have need of "all these (good) things." It is God whom we praise, not the illness, war, and hunger.

Most suburban church groups have a certain limit on how personal and probing conversation is allowed to go. This might well be advisable unless the group is prepared to deal constructively with what would otherwise happen. George disobeyed the rules in his group, however, when testimonies were being given about dark clouds having silver linings. The wife of a man in a wheelchair said that through the crippling of polio, they had come to a deeper faith than anything they had previously known. George said that these two persons obviously value this faith above all things and wanted to know, therefore, if they were grateful for the disease.

This was no intellectual smart talk on the part of George. With considerable ability and a bright mind, he was unable to make it in society. He called himself an emotional cripple, unable to continue in college, unable to hold a job, and unable to keep his family together. His painful probing of the couple and of himself took the form of a witness. Christians aren't called to praise disease. We hate disease just as other people hate it and try to eliminate it, even if it is the occasion through which we come into a new and deeper appreciation for life. Remember that others have the same disease and emerge bitter and cynical. Tragic and painful experience is no guarantee that we will receive new life. We praise the One, George said, who can use our most dreaded experience as an occasion to provide new life and joy.

We say to our children, "Don't be unhappy that you do

87

not have a new dress. Think of the children in the world that have no clothes at all." This is a sobering thought to adults, but it is usually lost on children, and it certainly raises the question of what we would say if we were the parents of one of those naked children. We might say, "Don't be unhappy that you have no clothes. Think of the children whose bodies are so infected that they can wear no clothes." But where does this end? In Christian worship we praise God for his acts of love by which he gives fulfillment regardless of one's state—rich, poor, or whatever.

This was made personal for me as I lay in the hospital with facial paralysis. I did not know that it would eventually disappear; I knew only that I hated it. How could I, a pastor, continue my profession with such a condition? An attendant said, "Don't feel bad about your facial paralysis. Think of those persons whose whole bodies are paralyzed." Instead of providing comfort, his words caused me to be more resentful. I was sorry that other people were worse off than I. I really was. Maybe this kind of reminder can help others be grateful and offer praise, and maybe it might have made me grateful at some other time, but praise was a long way from what I was experiencing in those hours.

The content of praise in Christian worship that is directed at pastors with facial paralysis is the same as that offered to the secretary with the splitting headache or the man with terminal cancer. It is sub-Christian to thank God primarily because we are not as bad off as we might be. Rather, we praise God for his acts of love that transform our lives within every adversity, trivial or death-dealing, and within every time of happiness and fun as well. Christian worship lets the world know that there is One who loves this world and its creatures so much that he will overcome any obstacle to make his love known.

Praise is at the heart of Christian liturgy and it is grounded in reality, not wishful thinking. Christians do not celebrate that each cloud has a silver lining. Some clouds have storms in them and we know it. We don't have to lean on the quote, "It is always darkest just before dawn." We know that it is also darkest just before it becomes totally dark. We offer no Christian pronouncement to the person who is seriously ill in a hospital room by saying, "Cheer up, you will be well and back on your feet in no time." Some people do not get well and never stand on their feet again. The patient is aware of this. We do well to point to possibilities of healing and hope, but Christians praise the One who redeems us both in sickness and in health.

Proclaiming the Word

Proclamation is discussed in its various forms in some detail at other places in this book. Brief comments are given here to indicate its inclusion with praise as part of the middle section of a service. Along with praise we hear God's Word through the ancient witness of the Scriptures. Then the creed, as Edward Hobbs points out, symbolizes liturgically how tradition stands between Scripture and the word of contemporary witness. The witness or sermon is a statement of the relationship of the Christian faith to the present in the light of the biblical witness. It attempts to answer the question, what does it mean for me, today, to respond in faith through the everyday situations of my own existence?

Sermons are not biblical because they contain a given number of quotes from the Scriptures. Biblical preaching sets forth a witness in which life is presented through understandings consistent with the Bible understandings. This is no place for "I've always liked to think that man . . . ." How does the Bible speak of man? Interpretations vary, certainly, but Christian preaching of man, God, love, and all other subjects is grounded in the basic witness and stance of the Scriptures.

Another way to approach the content of the proclamation is to call it truth-telling. No other institution has the kind of freedom and mandate to tell what is really going on in our world. Mass media are unable to present the total story because of the built-in control which advertisers possess. The scientific community often forgets about truth in historical terms. The church, however, is called to tell the truth even if it costs it its own life, and much of its preaching must be directed against its own life. Preaching is not concerned with preserving any institution for the sake of the institution, including its own. Only the grace of God finally counts, not the institution that proclaims it.

The Christian Offering

The service of offering, the third and final section of worship, could be called the "amen" portion. The title would not mean "the end," as the word "amen" is sometimes misinterpreted, but rather would signify the New Testament meaning described in this book, namely, I not only hear the message but I also will make it my own. The call to commit ourselves to the gospel which we have been proclaiming in our liturgy is the content of this third section. We hold before ourselves the charge to place our lives where our words have been. This is the "going-forth" celebration of worship. Our biblical texts are unlimited—"Here am I! Send me." "Go thou and do likewise." "Faith without works is dead."

Offering—Act III—has received as little attention in our services of worship as has its corresponding seasons in the Christian year—Epiphany and Pentecost. It would be strange, however, if we were strong on this section. Jesus certainly dealt with the problem of those who say, "I go, Father," but do not go. The problem of words and no action is apparently a problem which the church will always face. Face it, it must. But it must face it realistically. The institutional church has never consisted mainly of doers.

. The only profanity I ever heard from a pastor friend of mine came in his description of the congregation that he served. He said that one small group wanted to do nothing but pray. Another small group wanted to do nothing but play. He said that the majority, however, really just didn't give a damn. His sentiments were not far from those of other pastors and lay leaders who are critical of the lack of action by the church.

Criticism from within and denunciations from outside point to the failure of the church's performance to measure up to its words, to show by its life that it means what it says. These judgments have been of the church since the beginning. The apostle Paul often expressed his concern about the churches' failure to "also walk by the Spirit." We don't excuse the church, of course, by saying that this is just its nature. The gospel reminds us that each refusal to respond in action to the claim of the Christian faith is the decision to choose death instead of life, whether it be a corporate or an individual refusal. Our mistake is not that we judge the church too severely. Rather, we have been spending our energies foolishly combating waste trivia instead of involving ourselves in those areas in which we can bring significant change.

A Look at the Criticism

The institutional church ought always to expect harsh criticism. How, for example, can we expect mass appreciation for the church in society even when we are truly being the body of Christ? The writer of Ephesians says that we, the church, are the body of Christ. Are we so deceived by thoughts of a world getting better and better that we have convinced ourselves that our generation responds differently to Christ than did those persons who crucified him almost two thousand years ago? The accusations hurled at Jesus and his disciples included a heavy emphasis on their failure to be "religious" people, referring to their working on the sabbath, etc. The people knew what it meant to identify God, for they had met him in Moses, in Abraham, and in Isaac. Today, we, too, identify God by pronouncing as holy the past forms in which he revealed himself. This is what it means to be enslaved by the law instead of living in the freedom of God's grace. Christ did not come to destroy the law, for law in this sense is the body of past revelation. It was valid revelation, it was from God, but it is past. The world condemns the church even when it is truly being the body of Christ because society always interprets fresh revelation, the action by which Christ comes to "fulfill the law," as being a failure to live up to the true faith.

It is also impossible for the church to measure up because of the conflicting norms that various groups use. We can get a clear picture of what is always happening in the church by looking at the sharp projection of this dilemma through the history of the German church during World War II. Members of the church saw the evil that was taking place. Attempts to deal with this in the context of the church, however, were resisted by many of those persons who, in fact, were opposed to Hitler. They believed that the church measures up to its words when it stays out of political and social concerns, centering its attention on prayer and hymn-singing.

On the other hand, many members and nonmembers

regard any time spent elsewhere than in the realm of social action to be at best wasted and, at worst, an abomination to the Lord. Even though their whole lives reflect liturgy of one form or other, they are impatient with the church's liturgy. Religious liberals are strong at constructing symbols, creating songs, writing slogans, and wearing particular garb in reference to worthwhile causes for justice. They are wise in their pursuits. Most causes would not make much of a witness without at least some of these. Many such persons, however, somehow fail to relate this same understanding of the vital role of the prayers, hymns, and creeds of the church to the work of the church in the world. They condemn the church for not measuring up to its words and at the same time condemn it for spending time proclaiming publicly the Word to which it is called to bear witness.

Even if we were to agree on what the church is about and what its true role is, why should we expect the majority to be hard at work in it? To condemn society or any institution for being apathetic, to reject the institutional church because only a portion of its members are really committed to its task, is to flail away at a fact of life. Jesus makes it clear that the way is narrow and that those who follow it are few. No event in history which created a more humane society was brought about by the masses going to work on the problem. Reforms are initiated by a relatively small number of dedicated persons, and these few must bring them into being. What better model do we have of this than the whole biblical witness—the Israelites and the followers of the cross?

God's Power with *What Is*

God does not give up on anyone, nor does he write off a segment of any society or any nation. To recognize our dependence on individuals and minorities for significant action is not a giving up on people. We do not dismiss our calling to go into all the world to take the Good News by admitting the inertia of the majority of people. Jesus' statement that we will have wars and rumors of wars was no resigned acceptance of violence and killing. He was not speaking fatalistically, for it is he who also reminded us that it is the peacemakers who are called the children of God. His call was for followers to deal with the real situation rather than a pretended future that was not going to be.

We are not in any way without hope in this stance. We believe that God can and does bring redemption in a world of apathy and does not withhold his gift until we have purified ourselves or made the world a better place in which to live. "While we were yet sinners, Christ died for us." Those who cannot accept this dynamic understanding of life and who believe that they can bring into being a world which will know only kindness and compassion are headed only for disillusionment and ultimate cynicism. "Even if we know that we really won't bring in this ideal world, we have to make ourselves believe it or else we would all quit work." Not so for the Christian. He understands the futility of achieving a perfect world. Utopias are always tyrannies which destroy man's freedom. But he knows that every act of love and ministry to his neighbor, both individually and through the structures of society, counts infinitely. He will not be finally discouraged about the "results" or lack of "results" of man's efforts. He trusts God's promise and knows that the One who created us will also redeem us and our world, even in our most deplorable state.

This final section of offering is charged with the responsibility of helping the worshiper understand and express the content of his dedication to God in a realistic way. It attempts to set forth the content of the Christian's response to God's presence, to tell what it has meant and what it will mean for one to live each day in faith. But will we really go forth in action, back into our daily lives to live each moment in total obedience to the gospel? Only at times. No wonder others see us as hypocrites. We are indeed hypocrites in so many ways, but not because we enter into the drama of worship knowing that in our daily living we shall not fully respond to its claims. This, in fact, brings us back again to confession—the life-style of all Christians.

Offering Our Critical Judgment

The content of offering is our willingness to trust our lives to God. We make our daily decisions with maximum use of the intelligence God has given us, a knowledge of our conditions, and whatever sensitivity we have, knowing that our acts may bring loss instead of gain. We do not need to know how history will interpret our action. God calls us to be faithful in love, not perfect in knowledge. We can decide and we can know that "it will be all right."

A woman in the church was telling a friend about her difficulty in making a decision. Should she or should she not let her daughter take a two-week bus trip with other youth? She was quite anxious about the decision, but her friend told her, "Certainly something might happen to your daughter, but it will be all right. You can trust God." The woman with the decision was even more perplexed. Was the friend saying that the daughter might indeed be injured or killed on the trip but that everything would be all right? She wasn't looking for a way to handle tragedy at the moment, but rather was struggling with a decision whether the risk of danger involved in the trip outweighed the benefits that her daughter might receive from going. God was calling her to make as wise a decision as possible. If the risks seemed

95

minimal compared to the advantages, then she could make her decision to let her go, and at that point, and only then, she could trust that God would redeem any event that occurred.

This is what trusting our lives to God includes. We commit ourselves to him without minimizing our responsibility to make the best decisions we can make. Trust in God is no substitute for full use of all the critical powers he has given us. Having done all, however, we can then stand.

7

Communicating the Reality

Adequate communication is a prime concern of our age. It is no less a concern for the church. We want to know how we can better express our faith within the service of worship. The liturgical forms of the past—creeds, hymns, prayers, and the order itself—still have great meaning to some, but others are impatient with them. They see the church's traditional liturgy as a relic of the past that should be relegated to religious museums. "Relevancy" is our need. Others, however, see the task of the church at worship to be a matter of "holding the line." A struggle between relevancy and holding the line is the wrong battle. Rather than ask first if our language and forms are relevant or if they are unchanged from the past, we ask if they are true, if they are worthwhile, and if they provide the best possible means of communicating the gospel.

The Past and the Present

Learn what the language and forms of the past were saying and why. This is a good beginning for improved communication. Many contemporary worship forms are empty and are headed in directions which miss the vital proclamations of the faith (if they do not, in fact, pervert them) because they are born out of ignorance. We are too impatient to examine the content and the understanding which produced particular approaches in the traditional liturgy. Some serious study, therefore, of the content and rationale of those worship acts of the past centuries can provide the base from which newer forms can be considered. Some of the persons most excited about liturgy today are those who have done the homework just mentioned and realized the liveliness and power of these old forms and phrases. The primary reason that most of our traditional liturgy is rejected is not because it is worn out or otherwise inappropriate for our day, but rather because we have not made the effort to understand it. It is being rejected, however, by such great numbers that this is no time to sit around and cry about what might be. We live in *this* time and are therefore charged with the responsibility of finding clear and vivid means by which today's congregation can express the historic Christian faith so vital to our immediate lives.

A second demand on us is an awareness of what the means of modern media about us have to offer. We may decide, for example, that films are "in" on Sunday morning and put together a slide presentation to serve as the sermon, but many such efforts are failures. They fail for several reasons, and the first is a lack of knowledge of how such an undertaking can best be done. The availability and popularity of multimedia do not replace hard work and planning. Do-it-yourself types are not to be discouraged, for this is not a "professionals only" kind of field, but we can't hope for technical devices to make the planning of liturgy easier. Their function is to make worship more vivid.

What Are the Needs?

Contemporary efforts fail also because they are planned without a strong image in mind of who the worshipers are to be. The pastor and laymen who plan worship need to name names of those who will be present. Will this speak to C. L. and his sons? Evelyn will be there; how is it that the Word best comes through to her? We aren't necessarily asking if they will agree with it. We want to know if it will be a viable means for them in the expression of the gospel. Worship planning in a local church needs to be done by those who are most sensitive to the lives of the members. The failure of the jazz mass to be received in a number of instances occurred because jazz was not a familiar form for the people with whom it was done. The fact that jazz is America's contribution to the world of music does not mean that it is listened to, appreciated, or understood by all church members or even the majority of Americans. This is especially true of "modern" jazz. The jazz mass is an important contribution to the church, but it could be one of the last forms to communicate in a particular local congregation.

Folk singing is in much the same situation. Although it is quite popular with segments of people in our nation, some of our population do not listen to it and they know the performers only through the headlines in the papers. The tensions, contrasts, and other qualities of hard rock music could offer good reason for their inclusion in some way in the service. However, if most of the members of a church automatically reach for the dial when such music comes on their radio, how much more dislike is generated when these sounds come in church where the members cannot turn them off.

The contemporary form that is familiar to a great number in our society is a sort of "swing" approach that was so much a part of the 1940s. Certain country-western sounds and a calypso beat also seem to be appreciated and easily adapted by congregations. My point is, just because it is new, just because it is "in" with some, does not mean that it will be more workable with the majority of people than some of the music of past centuries. We don't limit ourselves, therefore, only to those idioms that are familiar,

We might decide to employ approaches that are quite un-familiar, but we need to be aware of what we are doing and who the people are with whom we are working. This is true of all means of communication, not just music.

The Levels of Language

Those who plan liturgy with a sensitivity as to how it communicates are wisely giving increasing attention to non-verbal forms. Regardless of how effective we discover these additional means of expression to be, however, we continue to be basically verbal. The language we use, therefore, is an important matter. We want words and phrases which provide the richest possible expressions of the Christian faith. Such language can be discovered and identified only as we become aware that we employ various orders in our speaking, all of which are appropriate to certain situations.

Aware of the objectionable features in the use of the following titles, I nevertheless believe that we will be helped by considering language basically as (1) symbolic or (2) literal. Liturgy is primarily symbolic language.

Symbolic language is the "how wonderful" and the "how terrible" form of expression. We use it inside and outside the church. Even in a time of great emphasis on analyzing all that is said or done, we still have a world in which symbolic language is in constant use in our daily conversations. It is poetic expression. It is the mythological, and it is the power and glory of much of our verbal exchange. Do not subject it to scientific examination. We exclaim, "The news sent me spinning." "I was floating on air the rest of the day." "You are really the most." "I was dissolved." "I went into orbit."

The Bible is full of symbolic language. Sophisticated men

100

take pride in having outgrown the ridiculous stories of the Bible, knowing that they really couldn't be true. But this is only to reveal our ignorance of the multiple functions of language. One pastor was able to solicit enough money to purchase six weekly radio programs for the purpose of defending the "truth" of the creation story against a scientist. What a waste of time! The Bible has nothing to defend. The pastor reduced the great poetic and mythological affirmations of this marvelous story to literal, scientific language. He saw himself in the role of a defender against modern scientism, but quite ironically, the very form of his defense vitiated his intention. He erroneously supposed that scientific language is the only way of speaking. Both he and the scientist read Scripture out of identical presuppositions.

Both men have been misled into believing that truth can only be verified by modern scientific method and reasoning. Both make their final appeal for validity of the Scriptures to tangible, measurable evidence, and fail to understand language levels—what words really mean to say. They do not appreciate the truth of stories, metaphors, and myths. When we probe deeply enough, we discover that the biblical literalist is really a modernist in that he settles for modern, scientific norms for verifying all truth. Literal language is an important and necessary language. The scientific method is a most appropriate one in those areas in which it is designed to function, but not elsewhere. We violate the Scriptures when we impose it on them.

For those who have difficulty with stories like the parting of the sea or the appearance of the star over Bethlehem, and who also want to retain their intellectual honesty and image of being a part of the modern world, a more acceptable approach is available. The parting of the sea is explained by wind, etc. The star over Bethlehem is really one that has now been identified by astronomers and will probably appear again within the next generation. Stop! This kind of talk might make some feel better about being able to retain belief in the Bible while also accepting modern science, but it misses the point entirely. The language is still being ill-treated as literal language instead of being understood in terms of its own intention. We have no reason to find embarrassment with the fantastic stories of the Bible or attempt to defend them scientifically. No language could be strong enough to express the overwhelming experiences of God's gift of love.

Bible films shown in our churches often turn out to be Trojan horses. They enter in the guise of revealing the Scriptures, but proceed to destroy the witness of the Scriptures by reducing these beautiful and powerful expressions of faith to physical events. Moviemakers would not consider filming contemporary stories and people in the reductionist and tragic way they have treated the Bible. What would they do in the filming of a life story of some famous man of our day if they discovered in their research a report that he "knocked them dead" with his speech in Iowa? How about a scene in which he "pulls the teeth" of his critics? Could inside cameras capture the butterflies in his stomach which he admitted having had prior to one occasion? If these illustrations seem ridiculous they only point to the greater ridiculousness and far more destructive treatment given the Scriptures by typical Bible films.

Liturgy also is primarily symbolic language. Not only does it include much expressive Scripture but it has also created some symbolic language of its own. The attempt to reword such language into literal, steno language too often results in thin, impoverished, prosaic hymns, creeds, and prayers. The loss in moving from symbolic language is not primarily an aesthetic loss, although this is a justifiable concern. What is lost is a dimension of life. The Apostles' and Nicene Creeds are not so much precise theological statements as they are testimonies, confessions, placards, hymns of adoration and celebration best carried and declaimed by the sublime music they have inspired for the great musical Masses. They are rightly called affirmations of faith, not descriptions of factual data. They are religious expressions, and I join those who claim that the church has always done much better with its religious language than it has with its theology.

Making It Plain

Rewriting liturgy is a risky business. It may well be an excellent educational exercise, but it is folly to think that we can find modern-day language which will make the creeds, for example, say "exactly what they mean." The hopelessness of the task is so apparent to some that without realizing the basic problem of mixed language, they set forth a brand new creed. The second failure of these efforts is their narrowness or provincialism. A close look at some of the "modern" creeds of a past generation reflects the kind of hopeful attitude of their day that man in his goodness will bring forth the kingdom. These creeds, like their accompanying hymns and prayers, did not speak of the Spirit as that which comes to judge, but rather the presence of one that only soothes. Instead of holding before us the major points of our faith with which centuries of the church have grappled, they reflected mainly the limited concerns of their own day.

A local church cannot afford to hold on to an ancient creed which is sound and solid, couched in tremendous language, if the congregation refuses to participate in that form of liturgy. What have we proved if we end up with a congregation consisting only of a pastor, a lay leader, and a professor of church worship? We can say, "We remained pure," but is this our calling? On the other hand, if the church sacrifices the integrity of the gospel it exists to proclaim, of what value is its continued existence? Fortunately, these two possibilities do not exhaust the alternatives. Those dedicated to the task of enabling the liturgy to communicate the Good News to our own generation will, with patient research and sensitivity, find ways of keeping it fresh and vivid. This chapter offers ways in which various churches are working to make such a witness.

Before liturgical illustrations are given, we need to remind ourselves of the most powerful way by which liturgy is communicated—the life-style of the congregation. Many persons outside the church figure out what the liturgy of a church is about by seeing how that congregation approaches its mission. I am not speaking of lapses and failures that occur in any congregation's life. But to what is the commitment of the congregation? Is it really willing to lay down its life? The best answer to what liturgy means is given by the direction in which the church is going. Whether or not we like the position or stance of a particular church, we can answer the question, "What do they mean by believing in God?" by saying, "The corporate life of that church provides the answer."

What to Do Till the Pastor Comes

These suggestions offer ways in which churches are proclaiming liturgically the historic faith within a changing society. They cover several areas of the service of worship, and their forms suggest still other uses. One of the best contemporary forms is an introductory statement prior to a call to worship or other "formal" beginning of the service. It can be given by the pastor but is better delivered by a layman. Brief words of introduction (approximately one minute) tell what is about to happen. Some point of the rationale for worship is presented: (1) we tell that we are about to have a drama and what it means to have drama in worship; (2) we suggest why expressive, poetic, symbolic language will be used at times; (3) we remind oursleves of those who will be worshiping in other churches, and include a sentence about the holy catholic church. The subject possibilities are endless. And if this work is faithfully done, during a twelve-month period the church could carry out a very significant program of worship education, both in the presentation of the statements and in the homework required for their presentation. If they are written, they will be more precise and can provide a handbook for the congregation. An example of such a statement is found in Chapter 8.

Judgment—Biblical and Now

Churches who precede the call to confession with scriptural words of judgment can add another dimension. The biblical sentences can be followed with words from contemporary sources which bring God's judgment on our society through life about us. Some careful work can tie the contemporary words with those from the Bible, but related or not, their function is to remind us that we dwell in the midst of a people of unclean lips. Examples are: (1) a feature story telling of the deplorable conditions in our state mental institutions; (2) a newspaper survey indicating our apathy in the design of our public buildings by not providing structural aids for people on crutches or in wheelchairs; (3) a news story on how a Negro soldier was unable to find mobile home space for his family prior to his leaving for Vietnam.

A story of a more personal connection might be given. A friend who is on welfare learns that her son in a correctional institution has lost his sight because of an uncared-for infection. She is unable to go to him because the hotel in the town where the institution is located does not serve people of a certain color. This is taking place, we are reminded, here in our own state.

The contemporary words can come through tape-recorded interviews made live with persons trapped in conditions imposed upon them by us. Taped excerpts from news reports, a live or taped statement from an attorney about unjust aspects of our legal system, and other verbal forms are ways of getting before us judgments on our corporate sins of which we ought to be made aware.

We also have nonverbal media. Large posters with photographs of those persons largely ignored by our society—the aged—could be carried silently through the congregation. The choir can present a contemporary anthem in which the text is one of judgment. Some churches might be able to arrange to show an appropriate film clip, or a brief movie such as those made by amateur moviemakers.

All these forms of contemporary judgment become the complement to the biblical words. They not only add their voice but also enable the congregation to grasp the scriptural pronouncements with a greater vividness.

I Believe in...

The affirmation of faith offers possibilities for retaining the traditional forms and yet bringing them into new life with contemporary approaches, utilizing both symbolic and literal language. Rather than attempting to rewrite the creeds, we could take the very first phrase and follow it with present-day statements read by laymen from where they are standing in the congregation. These laymen may have participated in the formulation of the statement. The affirmation is further improved if they also represent differences in sex and age. The congregation begins and ends the statement. Here is an example.

The Affirmation of Faith

All: I believe in God the Father Almighty, maker of heaven and earth.

First Reader: To believe in God is to be able to die and not to be embarrassed.

Second Reader: To believe in God is to have the great faith that somewhere, someone is not stupid.

Third Reader: To believe in God is to be one of those kids who just refuses to grow up and get older and older and die forever.[1]

All: To believe in God is to be those people who live in the knowledge that the possibility of really living can never be taken from us.

We can make a more theological affirmation of God by using the following witness:

The Affirmation of Faith

All: I believe in God the Father Almighty, maker of heaven and earth.

First Reader: What do we mean by the word God? Not less than this surely—the Source and Center of all being, the Determiner of destiny.

Second Reader: Reconciliation to God is reconciliation to life itself; love to the Creator is love of being, rejoicing in existence, in its source, totality, and particularity.

[1] Joseph Pintauro and Sister Mary Corita, *To Believe in God* (New York: Harper & Row, 1968).

All: Love to God is conviction that there is faithfulness at the heart of things: unity, reason, form, and meaning in the plurality of being. It is the *will* to maintain or assert this unity, form, and reason despite all appearances.[2]

Our Belief in Christ

The Christian year is a superb pattern for the creating and compiling of affirmations that will relate to the entire Apostles' Creed. We begin with Advent, for example, and affirm what it means to prepare for Jesus' coming.

The Affirmation of Faith

All: I believe in Jesus Christ our Lord.

First Reader: He comes to us as one unknown, without a name, as of old, by the lake-side, he came to those men who knew him not.

Second Reader: He speaks to us the same word: "Follow thou me!" and sets us to the tasks which he has to fulfill for our time.

All: He commands. And to those who obey him, whether they be wise or simple, he will reveal himself in the toils, the conflicts, the sufferings which they shall pass through in his fellowship, and, as an ineffable mystery, they shall learn in their own experience who he is.[3]

Another affirmation of our belief in Jesus Christ is more in the form of a theological supplement to the creed. This could be used in other Sundays of Advent or possibly more appropriately during Christmas or Eastertide.

[2] Adapted from H. Richard Niebuhr, *The Purpose of the Church and Its Ministry* (New York: Harper & Row, 1956), pp. 36-37.

[3] Albert Schweitzer, *The Quest of The Historical Jesus* (New York: The Macmillan Co., 1960), p. 403.

The Affirmation of Faith

All: I believe in Jesus Christ.

First Reader: Jesus collided with the lives of all he encountered. He invaded, broke into, penetrated their worlds, leaving them painfully unsettled.

Second Reader: To the proud he seemed humble and they were threatened. If men hated life, he loved it.

Third Reader: To those who hung desperately onto living, he appeared nonchalant about it all. If their living was a bondage, he was too obviously free.

Fourth Reader: Where men were other-directed, he was independent. Where they were confidently self-determining, he seemed lost in loyalties.

Fifth Reader: To conservatives he was manifestly revolutionary; he impressed the radicals as a reactionary.

All: The Christ decision is an election for or against life itself.

To follow in the steps of Jesus is not to imitate his words or reproduce his deeds. It is to be and do as a free man.

It is to walk out across the uncertain, ambiguous, anxious deeps of my life in gratitude, humility, and compassion, with the sure confidence that this very walking is the meaning of life.[4]

The next example represents a change in style not only in its supplemental material, but it also uses two phrases of the creed—one at the beginning and one at the end. The congregation's last response is vital if this unit is truly to represent an affirmation of faith.

The Affirmation of Faith

All: He comes to judge the quick and the dead.

First Reader: I was there, Jesus, as you know. I am part of

[4] Joseph Mathews, "Christ of History" (unpublished).

109

mankind, although I like to remember it only when I want something from my brother or society at large.

Second Reader: I shouted for your crucifixion, Jesus. I taunted you as you bore your cross, and I stood in the crowd to watch you die.

Third Reader: I am involved in your murder, Jesus, as in the lives and deaths of countless Jews.[5]

All: I believe in the forgiveness of sins. Amen.

Other Forms of Affirmation

All the supplemental material in these illustrations comes from outside sources. We can become even more immediately involved by encouraging original writing by members of our own congregation. Suggestions about laymen working in task groups on such a project can be found in Chapter 10. Concentration on symbolic language should not obscure our need to search for rich and powerful poetic forms to help communicate our faith. This is true whether the material is from outside or from within the congregation.

Nonverbal expressions can replace our words occasionally. Have the congregation say, for example, "I believe in the Resurrection of the body," and then show a brief movie which sets forth resurrection in scenes from today. A number of possibilities are available from film sections of public libraries as well as from commercial distributors.

A "poster parade" by boys and girls would involve the people even more. The constructing of Easter posters for such a parade could come out of an Eastertide study in an elementary-age class.

We can also follow a phrase of the creed with a hymn. Here is one suggestion.

[5] Malcolm Boyd, *Are You Running With Me, Jesus?* (New York: Holt, Rinehart and Winston, 1965), p. 37.

All: I believe in God.
All: (singing)
       My God, I love thee, not because
       I hope for heaven thereby,
       Nor yet because, if I love not,
       I must forever die.

       Thou, O my Jesus, thou didst me
       Upon the cross embrace;
       For me didst bear the nails and spear,
       And manifold disgrace;

       Then why, O blessed Jesus Christ,
       Should I not love thee well?
       Not for the sake of winning heaven,
       Nor of escaping hell;

       Not with the hope of gaining aught,
       Not seeking a reward;
       But as thyself hast loved me,
       O everloving Lord;

       So would I love thee, dearest Lord,
       And in thy praise will sing;
       Because thou art my loving God,
       And my eternal King. Amen.

Anthems do not have to be in the same place in the service each Sunday. Many anthem texts would serve beautifully as a contemporary accompaniment to any number of proclamations from the creed because of their poetic forms.

Acts of Praise

Our acts of praise usually include psalms. Rather than struggle to find new words for them, we can substitute contemporary words of praise at occasional services. The following example puzzled me when I first selected it for a Sunday morning. What if our weather did not provide a "blue true dream of sky" the words of this poem talk about? I suddenly remembered. "Of course, that is part of worship—

to be able to thank God for blue skies when we can see only dark clouds."

Words of Praise and Thanksgiving

All: i thank You God for most this amazing
day:for the leaping greenly spirits of trees
and a blue true dream of sky;and for everything
which is natural which is infinite which is yes

Minister: (i who have died am alive again today,
and this is the sun's birthday;this is the birth
day of life and of love and wings:and of the gay
great happening illimitably earth)

how should tasting touching hearing seeing
breathing any—lifted from the no
of all nothing—human merely being
doubt unimaginable You?

All: (now the ears of my ears awake and
now the eyes of my ears are opened)[6]

The Contemporary Lesson

We have a rich source for our last area of illustrations—"The Contemporary Word." Modern-day parables, excerpts from outstanding sermons, editorials, essays, poetry, concise and vivid statements from theological writings, and other verbal expressions are available to be placed alongside a Scripture lesson.

The following excerpt from a novel gives unusually direct parallel to the Lazarus story in the Gospel of John to which it refers. The story takes place among refugees in the moun-

[6] Copyright, 1950, by E. E. Cummings. Reprinted from his volume *Poems 1923-1954* by permission of Harcourt Brace Jovanovich Inc.

tains of Italy during World War II. It is winter and the early darkness finds the group lacking in activities. Michele, a member of the group, offers to read to them. They accept.

Michele took a little book from his pocket and said: "Cesira wanted a love story and that's just exactly what I'm going to read." One of the women . . . asked if it was a thing that had really happened or if it had been invented; and he replied that possibly it had been invented; but it was just as though it had really happened. . . .

The further Michele progressed in his reading, the more the faces of the peasants around him expressed indifference and disappointment. They had expected a nice love story; instead of which Michele was reading them the story of a miracle which —at least, as far as I could gather—they did not believe, any more than Michele himself believed in it. But there was a difference. They were bored—so much so that two of the women started chattering together again and quietly laughing, and the third one did nothing but yawn, and Paride himself, who seemed the most attentive of all, displayed an expression of obtuseness and insensibility. The difference was that Michele appeared to be truly moved by this miracle in which he did not believe. In fact, when he came to the sentence: "And Jesus said, I am the resurrection and the life," he broke off a moment and could not go on because he was crying. I realized he was crying because of what he was reading and that it was all related in some way to our present situation, but one of the bored women inquired anxiously: "Is the smoke troubling you, Michele? There's always too much smoke in here. . . . But of course this is only a hut." This woman was anxious to make excuses to Michele for the smoke, but he abruptly wiped away his tears and jumped up and cried: "Smoke indeed! Hut! That has nothing to do with it! I won't read to you any more because you people don't understand . . . and it's no use trying to make people understand who will never be able to understand. But remember this, now: each one of you is Lazarus . . . and in reading of you, Luisa, of you, Cesira, of you, Rosetta, and of myself too, and of my father and of that scoundrel Il Tonto and of Severino with his cloth and of the evacuees up here and of the Germans and the Fascists down in the valley, of everybody, in fact. You are all

113

dead, we are all dead and we think we're alive. As long as we think we're alive because we have our possessions, our fears, our trifling affairs, our families, our children, we shall be dead. Only on the day when we realize that we're dead, utterly dead, putrefied, decomposed, that we stink of corruption from a mile away, only then shall we begin to be just barely alive . . . Goodnight." He jumped up, upsetting and putting out the oil lamp and left the hut, banging the door behind him.[7]

Nonverbal means for our use include forms mentioned previously and also dramatic skits. One Sunday, for example, several could act out the story of the Good Samaritan following a reading of it from the Bible. When drama which is primarily spontaneous is used, it is essential that a beginning and an end be firmly in mind. That is to say, we need to be clear as to how we will come on stage and go off. The director appears and announces that he and several members of the congregation are going to present a variation of the Good Samaritan story. They are short one person, however, and will need to fill this vacancy in the cast at the end of the drama. Then, in a rather impromptu manner he sets the stage with the wounded man lying on the floor. Two or three contemporary passersby stop momentarily at the side of the wounded man. They explain, however, why it is that they will be unable to help. When they are gone, the director turns to two persons on the front row whom he has previously briefed. He says, "Which one of you will take the part of the Good Samaritan and help our friend?" One of the seated persons turns to the other and says, "You take the part—I don't know anything about acting." The other replies, "I don't know what to do; I would be embarrassed." After a few more similar excuses are offered, the director interrupts them. He says, "Never mind, the man just died."

[7] Alberto Moravia, *Two Women*. Reprinted by permission of Farrar, Straus, and Giroux, and Secker and Warburg.

Part III

Involvement
of the
Laity

8

Lay Participation in the Proclamation

The Christian church has always recognized the participation of lay persons in worship. After all, the first Christians were laymen—the church had no clergy. The extent to which laymen and laywomen have been involved throughout the church's history is a different story, however; so is the type of involvement. History has presented us with about every variation, ranging from services in which only the laity was involved to those in which the priest was unconcerned whether or not laymen were present when the Mass was said.

Talk and experiment in liturgy today are heavily weighted toward greater lay participation, even though most churches still do not reflect much change. Many laymen continue to see themselves as those who come to worship almost totally as receivers and as critics. A greater awareness of the ministry of the laity will need to be coupled with deeper understandings of the purpose of worship to help laymen move into a place of full citizenship in the service of worship. The theme of a great number of publications that came out in the early 60s calling for the layman to rise up and claim his heritage in the church will likely continue to be taken seriously as our total society moves closer toward grass-roots concepts. Therefore, despite the absence of any mass movement toward more involvement by laymen, the signs are encouraging.

The Christian faith is grounded in a basic conviction that all men stand the same before God. Ordination by the church neither guarantees nor prevents greater faith and it provides no deeper insights into God's word. Rather than minimizing the role of a pastor, however, this concept sets him free to serve the people in greater ways. His creatureliness is understood from the beginning by him and by the people, and he can proceed with the work of leadership without defensiveness. The layman who knows that he is no less a part of the church's ministry because he is not ordained will be less apt to compete with the pastor and more apt to assume a significant part of the total ministry.

Since the Reformation, non-Catholic churches have been regarded as examples of the priesthood of all believers, while the Roman Catholic Church was viewed as clergy-dominated. This does not hold up, however, especially in our day. A Methodist bishop, for example, has far more power over the clergy and laity than does a bishop of the Roman Catholic Church, mainly because the Methodist bishop has an assumed or understood power rather than an authority spelled out by the church. The moral double standards which Protestant laymen establish for free-church pastors certainly will match anything asked of priests. Even the extent to which laymen assist in the sacraments is more limited in some Protestant bodies than in the Roman Catholic Church.

The thought of a layman baptizing a child in a Protestant church never occurs to most of us. When no priest is immediately available and a child is in critical health, Catholic infants can be baptized by laymen. Such an act is strictly an emergency procedure, of course, and we further concede that their particular theology is at the heart of the emergency. Nevertheless, the layman is recognized as a valid minister in this extreme situation. For several years laymen have served on a regular basis as lay readers in the Mass. Even more significant is a change that now makes it possible for Roman Catholic laymen to minister Holy Communion. The authorization of who may do this is carefully defined, but this goes beyond the assisting role granted to many Protestants. Roman Catholic laymen can be authorized to assist the priest, but the most radical provision is permission for laymen to distribute the elements when no priest is immediately available. One need not advocate laymen performing baptisms or ministering the elements in order to call attention to the fallacy of characterizing Protestants as the lay-inclusive segment of the church.

Our concern is not which church does best, but what can we learn from one another. This is a prime time to look more closely at the real part which pastors and laymen have in Christ's church. We surely can't hide any longer behind such farces as Laymen's Day, in which we ask someone to do the preacher's job for one day. The very observance of Laymen's Day at worship once each year can be insulting and makes little more sense than a college remembering its students in special annual ceremonies. The laymen *are* the church—every day.

"On Stage" with the Pastor in Baptism and Holy Communion

One reasonable place to recognize the ministry of the laity and to help move toward greater recognition of such ministry is the service of worship. Later we can consider the laity's role in the planning of the service, but the service itself is a good place to see what "Every Sunday is Laymen's Sunday" might mean. Since baptism has too often been thought of as involving only the family and the pastor, it will serve well as a beginning place to point to some possibilities. Lay participation in baptism is encouraged in the liturgical reform of many denominations. The congregation's voice is included in the liturgy, publicly acknowledging responsibility for those being baptized itno the household of faith.

119

The congregation's participation is extended even further if a number of members come stand with those who ordinarily are at the place of baptism—the pastor, the one being baptized, and the family (in instances of infant baptism). The role of the Christian community is now more powerfully dramatized by the people surrounding the one being baptized, standing on all sides of him, "wrapping themselves around him." Laymen are further involved if a baptismal banner which they have made is displayed during the service. It might even be "custom created" for this particular person or persons.

The sacrament of Holy Communion offers the possibility of action beyond anything else in our liturgy. The coming to the table and kneeling as well as eating and drinking call for the involvement of the laity in an excellent way. Congregations have provided still further participation of laymen by restoring the practice of the communicant responding with "amen" when the words "the body of Christ" and "the blood of Christ" are spoken by the celebrant.

Laymen have also found greater possibilities of leadership in Holy Communion services. Here is one example. The Communion stewards may have placed the cloth on the table prior to the service, much like the practice of having the tablecloth in place in a home when guests arrive for dinner. The elements, however, are not on the table at this time. Then during the hymn of offering, the stewards bring the elements forward and place them on the table as part of the congregation's offering. The laity can be further involved by assisting in ministering the bread and wine.

Let the People Shout "Amen!" ("We dig it!")

People can also be involved by one simple little word— "amen." "We dig it" might be the best popular translation of this ancient liturgical response. Few words offered us by the youth are as unique and as untranslatable as the term "dig." It combines the cognitive and conative. If I dig what is said, I not only give intellectual assent but I am also committed to and bound by it. "Amen" means this. Members of the congregation have an opportunity to become a part of any prayer or other act by responding with "Amen." The clergyman or person offering the prayer never used the term in the earlier Jewish congregations. "Amen" was shouted only by the people as an occasion for identifying with what the leader had said or done.[1] The practice has carried into churches today primarily with the sermon, but it is also being recovered in wider ways. More people want to be a part of the service and more pastors are eager for the people to supplement their solo voices.

A minor extension came with the multivoiced choir offering a threefold or sevenfold amen. The response has been broadened far more, fortunately, by some pastors and congregations to include everyone present. The spoken "amen" is not as pretty as the four-part rendition by the choir, but other occasions can provide opportunity for choral offerings. Let the people shout "amen" at the conclusion of prayers, sermons, Scripture readings, or other such points in the service.

Take It from the Top

The role of laymen and that of pastors can be set forth rather dramatically in an act that also serves literally to call the congregation to worship. The lay leader, senior warden, chairman of the Board of Deacons, or some other

[1] Gerhard Delling, *Worship in the New Testament* (Philadelphia: Westminster Press, 1962), pp. 73-74.

lay person is the first voice heard in the service. He stands before the people and makes a brief statement of what the congregation is about to do. In approximately sixty seconds, which need in no way seem hurried, he holds up only one aspect of what the church, and especially that particular congregation, understands itself to be about in this service which is to follow. This would be different each Sunday. An example of this is the following:

Probably the most common charge leveled against church-goers by those who stay away on Sunday morning is that of hypocrisy. Do you think nonchurch people are being fair when they accuse us of coming on Sunday morning to pretend we are someone that we really aren't? Do we appear at worship services as a pretense of moral purity, trying to say that we are the "good guys"?

Certainly we do. At least in part. And not only is the charge of being hypocrites on target, but we are guilty of so many more selfish reasons for being here. These are not insignificant charges, and pleading guilty with a nod and a shrug is not *Christian* confession. We are here to acknowledge our failures, but we are also here to do much more! We have come to act out, to dramatize, to hear, watch, speak, and point to that life of freedom by which we are made alive! We gather to proclaim the Good News. Let all know that we are forgiven, accepted, and made whole through God's grace. This is what the service of worship this morning is all about.

At the conclusion of his statement a further action could follow. If the pastor is already in the sanctuary, he might stand or walk to meet the lay leader, who would then place a stole or some type of vestment on the pastor's shoulders. This communicates how the whole church, dramatized in the lay leader, commissions the pastor to function as leader of this priesthood. This might be even more vivid if the pastor is sitting in the congregation in street clothes prior to this act.

The lay leader represents the total laity further by being on hand at the end of the service to stand with those who have been received into the church (included in the liturgy of some denominations) or to stand by the pastor in offering a word to those leaving the service. In a sense he serves as "chairman" of the service with his presence at the beginning and the end. The pastor provides the professional role of leadership to which he has been appointed and for which he has been and is being trained. His job is not to push laymen into a spectator category.

The Sermon—on Behalf of the People

Following the murder of President John F. Kennedy in 1963, my memorial sermon made vividly clear to me what I had suspected for a long time. Those who crowded into local churches on those occasions came in part to hear something said that would make sense out of this absurd assassination event. Both consciously and unconsciously many came to participate in the total liturgy, to participate in all the acts of the church's worship as the media in which in this time of tragedy God's Good News is proclaimed. The sermon, however, was the point at which I became acutely aware of another reason for their coming. Laymen need the pastor to speak directly in contemporary prose *on behalf of them*. In an important sense, the people, not the pastor, create the sermon.

People who have been at work trying to understand the Christian faith and who have listened to the events of the world about them may not hear much that is new on Sunday morning. But the sermon is more than new insights from the pastor or the relaying of new information. The pastor takes the world and local community events, grapples with the Scriptures in the light of these events, applies his

123

theological understanding, and becomes the voice of the congregation after putting it together.

Bishop James Pike once told a group of ministers that a major portion of sermon preparation must be the conversation which the pastor has with laymen during the week. He receives from the people the witness they make to the gospel and includes their contributions in the proclamation each Sunday morning.

For laymen who recognize their contributions and the contributions of others, the sermon provides an additional way of lay participation. The pulpit message is not simply a summary of popular opinions, nor will the sermon necessarily be in agreement with the majority of views that have been expressed or are felt. But the sermon is understood to have come out of the kinds of questions and concerns that are a distinct part of daily lives.

One church has a plan in which a group of laymen meet with the pastor each week to participate formally in sermon preparation. Using the Scripture lessons of that church's lectionary, the laymen read the text, and all offer suggestions of what they hear in the Scriptures and discuss each other's statements. The pastor directs the discussion and takes final responsibility for constructing the sermon for Sunday morning presentation. The lay committee members are very certain, however, that they are an important part of what comes into being.

If a pastor does not follow the lectionary or if he is willing to vary from it, he sometimes finds that laymen want to hear him preach about a certain subject. Many would like private conversations on their questions, but preaching is complimented by being the preferred medium through which some want understandings dealt with. Without necessarily approaching the laymen with "What do you want me to preach about?" the alert pastor communicates by his style that he is open to such requests and that he will certainly make every effort to preach on a requested subject as soon as it is feasible.

Dialogue and Talk-Back

A more obvious way in which laymen may participate in the sermon is the practice of a lay person taking a role in dialogue preaching. He and the pastor, along with other laymen, work together in advance on the format and content. They could offer the sermon on Sunday in a kind of question-answer approach. The inquiring layman asks, for example, "How can theologians say that God is all good and all powerful and yet we have evil in the world? Is God not powerful enough to overcome evil or is he powerful enough but not that concerned?" The pastor then replies. But the pastor must also be the one who asks and the layman also helps provide an answer. This approach can, and quite often does, come off sounding quite phony, especially if one or both is representing a view that really isn't his own.

A highly appreciated dialogue comes from two persons who have similar concerns and theological orientations as well as similarity in sermon preparation and delivery. They confer during the week on the subject matter, telling each other some of the points that need to be made, relating illustrations, and finally agreeing on how they will begin and on what note they plan to conclude. When the preaching time comes, the pastor stays clear of any pretense that this is a conversation they just happen to be drifting into. He could say, "My friend Zan and I have been talking this week about what reconciliation means in terms of the Christian faith. We are going to tell some of what has come out of our conversations and want you in the congregation to

125

add anything you would like when we have said a few of these things. Zan, let's begin with that great story you were telling me about your childhood. . . ."

This approach can be a combination of both dialogue preaching and talk-back. Some pastors preach a solo sermon and then open the subject to the congregation. We need to consider at least two talk-back concerns. First, the hour together is a celebration, a proclamation of the gospel. We can save opposition and disagreement for an education class or other important free-for-all sessions. Remarks following the sermon are to be additional words of witness which the members of the congregation wish to add to what has just been preached. Arguments are helpful later.

Secondly, members need to know that this talk-back approach will be used, and they need information about what subject will be dealt with in order for them to be prepared. Even if members of the congregation have pertinent thoughts to offer, the prospect of speaking them on Sunday morning can be quite terrifying. If specific persons are contacted in advance and have agreed to talk back after the sermon, it should be made clear to the congregation that this has been done. No pretense at spontaneity is needed or appropriate. If additional witnesses are made on a spontaneous basis, they are more than welcome.

"Conventional" preaching has been written off too soon. It might be sick or even dead in some areas, but a twenty-minute sermon delivered by the pastor is the most significant communication some persons have all week, even in this day of cool multimedia. If the pastor doesn't waste time preaching on answers to unasked questions and if he truly brings the Christian faith to bear on today's life, the laymen will consider it very much their expression, even if they don't open their mouths.

126

Expanding the Choir

New dimensions of church music are with us. One which is most welcome but still much too seldom enjoyed is the participation of the congregation in certain parts of the anthem. Members of the congregation who are not in the choir should be given opportunity to make their joyful noise unto the Lord. Hymns are fine, but how much more exciting it is to be allowed to join in the anthem now and then.

Music can be expanded to more of the laity by welcoming those who want to add their talent even though it is not professional in quality. A children's rhythm band, for example, can be the accompaniment for a simple hymn. With a little imagination the person who directs the music can find ways of involving budding pianists or cornet players to participate in the regular service instead of including them only when a special children's program is given. The musical quality may suffer slightly on these occasions, but the benefits to the congregation as well as to the "artists" can be worth it.

Weddings—One Thousand Miles to Be a Spectator

A groom-to-be in planning his wedding said, "We want to include the congregation in this service. I recently traveled one thousand miles to attend the wedding of a friend and all I did was sit there. I didn't even get to say the Lord's Prayer; it was done by a soloist." The Order for the Service of Marriage isn't even included in the liturgy section of the United Methodist Book of Hymns because the congregation is basically present only as spectators. But many brides and grooms have not been content with this arrangement. Through assistance from pastors and other laymen, wedding

127

parties have created some really fine services of worship with the wedding vows in the center.

The following service is an example of a simple wedding service in which congregational participation was encouraged. This was one of the most appreciated and enjoyed weddings I have attended. With the chairs arranged in a semicircle about the altar-table, the service began with the hymn "Now Thank We All Our God." The congregation stood and sang as the groom and his family came to the front row of chairs on one side and the bride and her family to the front row of the other side. Following the hymn all were seated and the pastor made a statement. He told of the meaning of wedding gifts and suggested that members of the congregation might at that time offer verbal gifts to the couple. Some of the people present, he explained, were involved in the planning of the service and had already expressed their desire to have a part. Everyone was invited to speak. Nobody needed to feel obligated to do so.

The response was extensive. Expressions of love and friendship, wishes of health and patience, reminders of some of the meanings of Christian marriage, promises of support, and even a song with guitar accompaniment by the best man were presented. Some spoke with smiles and some spoke through tears, but the couple received all these wedding gifts with gratitude. The pastor then offered his gift in the form of a brief sermon.

The vows followed and were those of traditional liturgy. The couple had no problem about a traditional wedding service for they understood this service to relate them to all those who have exchanged similar vows in the great tradition of the holy catholic church.

Couples who are writing their own vows—and more are doing this—do reflect a concern and seriousness about their weddings, but most are poorly equipped to write vows which reflect the Christian understanding. Rewriting the liturgy is discussed in another chapter, but the point might be made here that the need to rewrite the vows ordinarily comes about because of a lack of understanding of the wedding liturgy and even the meaning of liturgy itself. "Contemporary" wedding services also usually lack the very concern of the preceding paragraphs—the involvement of the congregation in the wedding.

Sunday Morning Weddings

A service of marriage integrated into the weekly service of worship offers an unusually fine possibility for lay participation. Families and friends join the regular congregation in the celebration. Rather than intruding or interfering with the weekly service, the wedding actually illustrates the wholeness of Christian liturgy. As in baptism, our hymns, prayers, and Scripture readings are intentionally directed to a particular theme. On this occasion we celebrate human relatedness, particularly in marriage.

The first hymn becomes the processional during which the man and woman enter, along with their attendants, and stand with their respective families. They participate fully in the complete service along with others in the congregation until the singing of a hymn during the last section of the order—the time of offering. At this point they meet at the altar-table for the specific order of marriage. If the service is one of Holy Communion, the vows are exchanged prior to their receiving the elements. The last hymn is the recessional.

129

9

Lay Planning and Special Celebrations

Participation of the laity in worship means much more than additional voices or other contributions on Sunday morning. Most of the preceding has centered on what happens at the service itself, but some of it has also suggested how the whole people of God can be at work during the week in helping to bring the liturgy into greater power. Classes in the meaning of worship are important, but when concrete problems and interests are tackled, we often find unparalleled possibilities for real depth learning. The liturgy task group can be the vehicle through which laymen make this concrete approach.

The Liturgy Task Group

Any "how to" statement would certainly insist that the purpose and function of a liturgy task group must be very clear both to the pastor and to the members of the group if certain catastrophe is to be avoided. This is sound advice, but the very first task group with which I worked was so busy each meeting that it never quite got around to clearly determining and defining the purpose and function questions. Had I written earlier, therefore, the spelling-out of the nature of the group would have seemed of secondary significance. The second group was different. One session made the need for immediate identification and clarification of role most obvious.

Becoming informed with the basic meaning of worship is a most proper beginning. Instead of attempting to do all of the study first and working later on specific tasks of research, writing, etc., the groups move rather quickly into some practical applications. The task groups then move back and forth between theory and practice.

A Mod Good Friday Film

A good model for this approach is the experience of some senior high students in preparing an 8mm movie for Good Friday. The idea of the movie was fascinating. After one hour of "learning all about Christian doctrine," the class quickly moved into the planning session for the movie. The suggested theme of "What Crucifixion Looks Like Today" was acceptable to the youth, and they began brainstorming the scenes and sounds that would comprise their creation. Fortunately, but not accidentally, the leader was far better oriented in an understanding of Christian faith than he was in moviemaking.

As the boys and girls poured out almost endless ideas of what would make good footage, challenges began to come from each other. When the brainstorming slowed down, the suggestions were evaluated in seriousness. "Yes, but what has that to do with Jesus' Crucifixion?" "That misses the whole point." "Where did you get that kind of thinking?" Theology again reared its head. The rest of the time, especially the editing session and the afternoon spent in the creation of a sound track, was a constant exchange of theological reasons and justifications for what went in and what came out. The class was so convinced that the final product was an urgent word on how the crucifixion is related to today's world that they insisted on conducting a discussion period following the Good Friday showing.

Three Task Group Illustrations

Weddings, funerals, and baptisms are especially appropriate concerns for lay study and planning. Discussions about what ought to be done and what ought not to be done on these occasions can raise all kinds of questions and cause laymen to dig deep into the meaning of the Christian faith. Struggling with the "whys" of these special services can produce understandings beyond what might come from a series of lectures by experts. The following illustrations indicate how deeply and how significantly laymen can be involved in the heavy but highly rewarding work that lies behind the worship services of the church. The illustrations are: (1) The Wedding Statement; (2) The Funeral Statement; and (3) The Baptism Statement.

These three statements were written by laymen who volunteered their efforts. They constituted the task groups in which individual and small group assignments were made. When each group finished compiling and editing its work, the report was submitted to the Commission on Worship, which had been receiving regular reports. After further editing by the commission, the reports were presented to the Administrative Board. Minor refinements were made and the statements were duplicated and distributed to the entire congregation. Further distribution followed requests from other interested churches, groups, and individuals. A copy of the wedding statement is given as a matter of course to couples who come to the pastor for the planning of their wedding.

The creation of such statements can prove to be valuable experiences for churches. If the reports are basically the work of the pastor with fringe lay involvement, a major benefit will be lost. If uninformed laymen simply pool their preferences or prejudices, the results might be worse than no report at all. These are not the only alternatives, however. Plenty of time for lay research, conversations with professionals in liturgy if such are within reasonable distance, and close cooperation with the pastor are needed.

The Wedding Statement

Possibly the most significant aspect of this wedding statement is that it reflects the willingness of laymen to go beyond the superficial information that is to be found in any number of booklets and guides. The following paragraphs are excerpts from the statement.

The Meaning of Marriage

Marriage is the celebration of the arrival at a point in the lives of two individuals at which they decide to proclaim to society their desire to *formally* establish a marital union. Marriage does *not* begin (excepting the strictly legal aspects) with the vows of a civil or religious rite; rather, it is a developmental relational *process*. It is a *process* of union which begins with mutual acceptance in dating and continues beyond vow-taking in a growing understanding and interdependence.

Should a couple decide to proclaim their marriage in a religious rite, it should be clearly understood that vows do *not* magically make a marriage. The church's rite provides the couple an opportunity to witness to the community their desire to enter into a *responsible* union and to ask the church's recognition, response, and participation. In fact, it is the man and woman who are the "ministers" in the Service of Marriage. The clergyman (apart from his office as a "servant" of the state) is a representative "witness" who has been empowered, through his office, to bestow the church's blessing on the marriage; he does not, contrary to popular opinion, "marry" the couple.

A man and woman who decide to proclaim their marriage in a Christian rite have the exciting possibility of doing this in the context of the corporate worship of Almighty God.

Following this statement, the legal requirements as set forth by the state were outlined. A subcommittee gathered as much accurate, up-to-date information as possible concerning what constitutes a valid marriage, including minimum age restrictions, medical requirements, and who is authorized to sign the marriage license. Next came a statement which was one of the most difficult ones to word but which dealt with a frequent request—what to do in the case of divorced persons. Other excerpts follow.

We recognize the sincerity and reasoning of other denominations whose clergy refuse to marry persons who have been divorced. In some cases persons who have been refused the rites of marriage by one of these denominations will come to a United Methodist church. We do not feel that it is our purpose to keep the consciences of non-Methodist pastors clear; however, we base our decisions in these matters on the basis of now and the future rather than the past. We concur with the United Methodist position that divorce in itself is not sufficient reason to prohibit marriage.

Why a Christian Wedding

Since there are other legal and accepted ways of becoming married, a church ceremony is justified only when one or both persons are Christian church members and desire a service of worship. Non-Christians or those Christian couples who are determined to have a secular wedding (one with overemphasis on romantic, sentimental music, "impressive" decorations, flowers and clothing, no congregational participation, etc.) should consider renting a suitable hall and having a civil wedding. Since the vows are explicitly Christian vows, it would be a contradiction for a person to say, "through the church of Jesus Christ our Lord," or, "in the name of Jesus Christ"—openly identifying with Jesus Christ and the church—if the person had not made a public commitment to the Christian faith.

A Sample Service

Here is the outline of the sample service which is offered in much more detail in the statement. Almost every act calls for participation by the congregation.

The Worship of Almighty God on the Occasion of the Marriage of _____ and _____.
The Call to Worship
The Prayer for Purity
The Hymn
The Prayer of Confession
Words of Forgiveness
Versicle
The Venite
The Word
  First Scripture Lesson
  Anthem or Special Music
  Second Scripture Lesson
  The Witness to the Word
The Hymn
The Service of Marriage
The Benediction

Music and Other Information

Music for weddings is considered in detail in the next section of the statement. Hymns, solos, and anthems together with organ or other instrumental preludes, processionals, and postludes are suggested and a statement is made about the meaning and place of music at weddings. A variety of other informational items are included—photograph limitations, costs, receptions, etc. The following statement indicates how some of these subjects are treated.

135

In choosing clothing for the wedding, it should be borne in mind that clothes are not the central concern and should not detract from the real meaning of the ceremony. Some thought should be given as to the appropriateness of the garments to accommodate the ceremonial activities (such as sitting or kneeling).

The festiveness of the wedding may be reflected in the decoration of the sanctuary, but always must be limited by the discipline of Christian worship. All decorations used in a service of worship should enhance the distinctive Christian symbols in the church. White paraments are used for weddings. Flowers, greenery, and candles should be kept to a minimum, and nothing is permitted which would detract from worship rather than enhance it. For example, there should be no flowers on the altar-table which is always appropriately reserved for the vessels used in Holy Communion. If there is no retable, flowers may be placed at either end of the altar-table or forward in the chancel area.

The Funeral Statement

The funeral service has been determined so extensively by the funeral director, the next of kin, and local customs that the church's voice and its liturgy have often been looked upon as an intrusion. Laymen who were very sensitive to this situation decided to do something about it, at the suggestion of the pastor. Beginning with a half-dozen members, the group eventually included three times that number.

The statement is obviously not a directive on "The Exact Way to Regard Death Christianly and Rules for Funerals," but it deals with specific matters with which Christians are concerned. Some of the sections represent near or completely unanimous opinions of the group while other sections had unresolved differences. These excerpts are from a revised statement. The continued need for revisions will undoubtedly be recognized.

Purpose of Statement

Central to the concern of the Christian church are the relationships of its members, both in their lives and at the time of death. Life and death matters are the questions dealt with in an understanding of what faith is all about. In our day the Christian church has been less mindful than in the past of its duty to instruct and to minister to its people before the time of death. We feel it is the church's duty to help people be as well-prepared as possible to deal in a Christian way with all the details which arise along with the questions and the sorrow of death. The purpose of this writing is to help people have some understanding ahead of the problems and decisions which will be theirs when death occurs. The following pages include information and some recommendations consistent with the church's understanding of what it is to live and die a life of faith.

Death as Reality

In our day "death" has often become a morbid word spoken in hushed tones or seldom mentioned at all among families and friends. But death is interwoven in the fabric of living, and should be an accepted part of our daily lives. There should be no skirting of the subject of death even with someone who has recently had a death in the family. There is a need for continuing discussion about the deceased person, the remembering of this life in reality—both the good and the bad.

The intense grief which comes at the time of death in the family is normal. The crying out against death is itself affirmation of the goodness of life. There is a mixture of selfishness and faith in this crying out. The security and the living habits on which we have depended for meaning are wrenched and torn from us. Grief at our loss is as valid as the grateful thanksgiving for the temporary gift of this individual life.

We are people of both faith and unfaith. We trust God fully only at times. We may commit our loved one to God truly one moment only to find ourselves beset by doubts a moment later.

Another thing should be said about our attitude toward

death. There is joy as well as sorrow in remembering the deceased together with friends and relatives. There is a place for laughter along with the tears in a house where death has occurred.

There has been a constantly growing attempt on the part of Americans in the past fifty years to evade the reality of death. Our great emphasis on youth and pleasure and materialistic possessions has made us afraid of the end of life and caused us to deny our faith. We have gratefully turned over the whole ritual of death to strangers and have expended vast sums hoping to free ourselves from getting near death. The funeral homes and cemeteries have met this demand with all the luxuries our society has requested. If the intention of expensive caskets, steel vaults, "perpetual" care cemeteries, artificial makeup and embalming, is to make the body seem alive or to keep it from decaying, then we have denied our biblical faith.

Christians do not need to deny the reality of death. They have the assurance and the experience of God's love here and now and the faith that God's love precedes them in life and in death. Christian faith continues to urge men to fully participate in all of life, in every relationship with every person. It even assures us that we may participate fully in our own illness and death with the sure knowledge of God's loving care.

If we trust God today in a willingness to risk commitment to him, then we can be unafraid of the future for ourselves and for our family and friends, trusting God ever more faithfully as we grow in grace. Our future is in his hands and we know we can trust him.

The question for a Christian is never what lies beyond the grave but who meets us on both sides of the grave—in life and in death. Detailed speculation about what happens to this person after death is unnecessary for the people of faith who believe that God is present in the time and place of death as surely as he has been in the past.

The Christian concern at the time of death is always with the living. The historical Christian community has always rallied around the surviving family, surrounding them with love and sharing fully in this time as with all the other important events of life. This sort of community needs to be recovered in our day so that we may truly be a part of the life of others in their great need.

Perhaps one of the most helpful ways to express concern at the time of death is the personal visit to the family of the deceased. It is unfortunate that we often avoid person-to-person contact with those most directly affected by death. We shy away from the grief of others because we are afraid to cope with it. The thought of visiting someone who has known the death of a loved one raises such questions as, "What can I say? How do I express my concern without adding to the sorrow already present?" We have felt these reservations at one time or another. As conscientious members of the church, we should strive to alleviate these restricting anxieties which often hold us back from fully responding to the needs of others at a time of death.

When visiting the bereaved, we will not always find the best expressions of concern simply in words. The death of someone close can release a wide range of inner feelings which need to be heard. Thus, our being good listeners is often more comforting than anything we might say.

There are no specific rules which tell us how to respond to the event of death. Each situation must be met on its own. The point is that *we have a responsibility to communicate our concern.* The personal visit is a good way of doing this. It is best if we can respond to a death in person.

One of the customs of our time in expressing concern and sympathy to the family of the deceased is to send flowers. This expression can be strengthening and supporting to the bereaved family, flowers being of great significance to some people in both the giving and the receiving. Other ways to communicate concern are telegrams and phone calls to those out of town. Perhaps a more lasting memorial to one who has died is to give money to an institution which furthers the ideals of the deceased. Among the many such organizations are one's church, a hospital, and medical research.

Funeral Service

The term "celebration" has often been used in Christian history to describe the worship of God in every situation. This phrase could well be reclaimed for the funeral service of worship in which we proclaim the love of God in relationship to the life of the deceased and his survivors. The term "celebration of God's love" applies to all common worship, whether the occasion be a baptism, a confirmation, a marriage, or a funeral.

The Christian community gathers without fully understanding death and without being able to provide answers to all the questions which death raises. Nevertheless, we come together to witness to the truth made plain to us by the cross, that neither suffering nor death nor any condition imaginable can defeat the love of God.

"For I am sure that neither death, nor life, nor angels, nor principalities, nor things present, nor things to come, nor powers, nor height, nor depth, nor anything else in all creation, will be able to separate us from the love of God in Christ Jesus our Lord." (Rom. 8:38-39.)

The Order of Worship

The family is reminded that funeral services should be held in the church and the Order of Worship proposed is basically that of the United Methodist *Book of Worship* used by the task group:

Call to Worship
Hymn
Prayer
Psalm
Gloria Patri
Affirmation of Faith
Scripture Lessons
Hymn
Sermon
Prayer
Benediction

The Open or Closed Casket

Probably the most controversial section for the group concerned the open or closed casket.

140

The Christian community gathers at the time of death for the worship of the Lord of both life and death. It is a time of full acknowledgment that death has occurred but also a strong declaration that this death can be entrusted to God and a re-affirming of the goodness of the life still offered us.

Some believe viewing the body is an important recognition of death and enables those who see the body to realize death has occurred. This act might be therapeutic and it might also be rather traumatic. Will this be an aid in the acceptance of death, or will the body as presented be an attempt to dissimulate death? The question of an open casket should be decided on the basis of the considerations presented in the first section of this statement. The Christian community asks, "Is this appropriate to the worship of Almighty God, or is it rather a dramatization of the body?" The closed casket present in the sanctuary could be a sufficient reminder of this person's death.

The church's decision, made on the basis of the first section of this paper, has to be "no" to an open casket at the service of worship, to focus the *gathered* community's attention on the praise of God, whom we in faith believe is the One to whom we entrust both our lives and our deaths.

Whatever the family decides about viewing the body before the service of worship, the casket should be closed before it is brought into the church, and remain closed.

Family Participation in the Service of Worship

Experiences of some members of the task group resulted in a statement relative to the involvement of the family of the deceased in the service of worship—sitting with the congregation, singing the hymns, praying the prayers, and affirming the faith. Suggestions about the family's involvement are offered in the following paragraph.

Symptomatic of the current attempts on the part of many to hide from the fact of death is the practice of discouraging close family members from active participation in the service of worship. They are present, to be sure, but in many instances only as spectators. We wish to affirm the right and need of family members for a full worship experience. Further, even though the eulogy of a past era has come into disfavor with many, we suggest that a memorial statement given or requested by the family might be included in the worship ritual.

The Funeral Pall

The funeral pall, a traditional church vestment, is a large cloth, possibly bearing Christian symbols such as the cross. It has been out of use in church funerals for some time, probably due to the current trend of flower-covered caskets and our tendency to attempt to hide the fact of death.

As stated in the section on the use of flowers, a Christian service of worship in a church sanctuary must use the meaningful symbols of the church in expressing faith in God, during life and at death. The pall-draped casket is a significant reminder of the reality of death, encouraging the congregation to fully realize this death and turn to full participation in proclaiming our commitment of this person in faith to God. Use of the pall also discourages emphasis on the simplicity or costliness of a casket since we believe we are equal before God.

Our church owns both a black pall and a white one. The use of black is an effort to combat attempts to avoid death. The presence of the casket is already a strong reminder, however. If the white pall with a large gold or red cross covers the casket, we are reminded not only of the reality of death but also of the victory which God gives in the midst of death.

The Service at the Grave

A good deal of concern was expressed over the graveside service. It was the opinion of some members of the task group that many people are not certain what the meaning of this is or of its relation to the funeral. In addition to their statement which is given in its complete form here, a more lengthy statement was included as an appendix.

The service at the grave has changed considerably even within the past twenty years. This change has come about in part by the funeral director's efforts to shorten and simplify the occasion for expedient reasons, and in part through a general change in our culture. Self-conscious theological reasons have had a part, but apparently this has been minor.

The need is not necessarily to lengthen the service. There is much to be said for a brief service in respect for the family. Certain changes in present trends might make the service longer, but our basic concern is not about length. We are concerned with more understanding and with more adequate planning.

The service in *The Book of Worship* sets forth a brief liturgy consisting of a statement of committal, Scripture sentences, and prayers. With the exception of the Lord's Prayer, all of this is said by the minister.

It is here that we should give consideration to wider participation. The placing of a handful of dirt into the grave by each person present might be considered.

As elsewhere the basic need is to be honest and real about what is taking place. Any attempt to keep the grave from looking like a grave should be rejected. It is only within very recent years that many families have left before the casket is lowered and covered with dirt. For whatever reasons someone stayed (to prevent body snatching, etc.), the witnessing of the actual burial could be of great importance to all. It is another way of symbolizing our accepting death and our affirming it.

Turning the graveside service over to a fraternal organization should be seriously questioned. Often this is a very awkward service; many times it is poorly done. But the basic objection is the one raised by a staunch member of the Masonic Lodge who expressed his great appreciation for his lodge and what it meant to him, but said that the funeral service is the church's service. Some pastors refuse to be tacked on to the service of another organization.

Although some could also question the appropriateness of military honors at a graveside service, it should be recognized that this is not a part of the liturgy. Even if the funeral is conducted by a military chaplain, it is still to be conducted according to the liturgy of his church. The military honors are added when desired. One can certainly say that they are never sentimental or unreal, for death's reality is made quite clear on such occasions.

143

Supplementary Information

The final portion of the statement deals with the legal requirements of the state, costs and services of funeral homes, memorial societies, and legal and financial arrangements.

The Baptism Statement

The following statement on baptism involved more of the pastor's participation than did that of the wedding or funeral statements. It is, nevertheless, basically a statement from the laymen. Here are excerpts:

Baptism is best celebrated by the total congregation, not by small groups in private gatherings. Rather than being inserted or tacked on to a Sunday morning service, it can be made an integral part of the complete liturgy, from the call to worship through the benediction.

The Meaning of Baptism

"Do you not know that all of us who have been baptized into Christ Jesus were baptized into his death? We were buried therefore with him by baptism into death, so that as Christ was raised from the dead by the glory of the Father, we too might walk in newness of life." (Rom. 6:3-4.)

Christian baptism is thus set forth in incredibly forceful and meaningful language in the New Testament. The new life in Christ, into which early believers were being initiated, seemed so rich and so filled with hope that ordinary words were not sufficient. Christian man believed he had been born again. That is, he believed his life had become radically new. His new life could not be explained by saying that something new had been added, a new patch to an old garment, that some commandments were taken away and some added; instead, the very foundations of his existence had *been relaid*, the former life

144

had been done away with, and all things had become new. Christian man could only think of himself as a *new man*, a new creation.

Or, you could say he had died and had been raised from death. The world of sin and death now no longer had dominion over him. Set free from the power of sin and death, he was now free indeed, free to live his authentic existence in the service of God and of his neighbor. Since God has made him his own, there is now no condemnation. And therefore he owes no man anything except to love one another. This is life, new life, salvation.

But best of all, this new life is of God. What man could not do for himself, God did. No man is his own father; no man can raise himself from the dead. Thus, that which happens to man in baptism is wholly of grace. And the new being which God bestows upon us is pure gift, having its beginning and end in his love.

Infant Baptism

It is for this reason that the practice of the church in baptizing its infants and children is so forthright a proclamation of the gospel. In this baptism it is made fully clear that *God seeks us before we seek him.* Long before we are conscious of God, we are loved of him and have his claim and demands on our lives. God's love for man precedes man's love for God. Even from our first breath, God names us his.

The central core of our faith is better set out in the baptism of infants than in the baptism of adults. The child has nothing to bring, no faith, no good works, not even a rational knowledge of God. He cannot speak and has to be brought forward, having no knowledge of what is happening to him. The child, therefore, comes to receive; and, in this sense, becomes the model for us. "Truly, I say to you, unless you turn and become like children, you will never enter the kingdom of heaven."

The act of baptism does not make the child a member of the church as church membership is now understood. Church membership is consummated in the Service of Confirmation when the child has become old enough to make a public confession of his personal acceptance of the vows of Christian discipleship made for him. This personal response *must* be made if the redemption that God has already effected is to come to its full meaning within us. It is as if, to use a coarse illustration, a hand is extended to a drowning man. The hand is extended without considering the merit of the person drowning. But unless the drowning man receives the hand, it might as well never have been extended. So the covenant is initiated by infant baptism and completed by confirmation.

These words help explain several other things about baptism:

1. The younger the child, the more vividly is the word of the gospel proclaimed.
2. This is not designed to be a "sweet" service. The use of any measures that might tend to express sentimentality rather than the message of the gospel is to be avoided.
3. The parent couple proclaims, in offering up their infant to the symbolic "death" of baptism, the sovereignty of God over the life of their child.
4. Baptism is an act of the Christian community. The entire congregation accepts seriously the responsibility it has in the life of the child and his family.
5. The Old Testament points to the close relationship between water symbolism and a renewed covenant between God and his people. The ritual of The United Methodist Church states: "Let every adult and the parents of every child to be baptized have the choice of sprinkling, pouring, or immersion."

A statement on baptism will be made more helpful if it includes suggestions for participation by the congregation within the service such as those found in Chapter 8. It also needs to include the richness of the biblical and ancient symbolism which deals with water and the rites associated with our present-day service.

10

Lay Planning in the Weekly Service

Laymen certainly are involved when they form task groups to work on weddings, funerals, baptisms, and even on sermons. However, if a church organizes a committee or a task group to work on the *entire* liturgy for Sunday morning's service, that church has made a far greater decision about lay leadership. It can and does happen. Churches are creating continuing committees which meet weekly with the pastor to plan Sunday's service, while others meet less frequently and concentrate on specific seasons of the Christian year. Pastors ordinarily become quite nervous about this whole liturgy committee idea, and understandably so, but such a group can make a tremendous contribution to the church's worship and to its overall life.

The Task Group Approach in Weekly Services

The success that one church has had with a committee to plan worship makes a strong argument in favor of regular weekly meetings throughout the year, but a liturgy task group has many advantages over the continuing committee. The Christian year, for example, is almost an invitation to a task group approach—a group that comes into being for a specific task, determines what it will need in order to accomplish its goal, sets its own time schedule, and dissolves itself when it finishes its job.

The two great dramas of the Christian faith that center in Christmas and Easter provide the kind of focal points that task groups thrive on. The church can concentrate on these two high points of worship and not waste time agonizing over how to get more people attending weekly planning sessions, and whether or not meetings should be held in the summer. The problem of how to bring new committee members up to date can be overcome. Laymen can be freed to become involved in other areas of the church's life at other periods during the year, and the "psychic fatigue" of the liturgy laborers can be reduced.

Launching a task group in early October will provide time to publicize and preplan following the Labor Day "New Year." Advent is still almost two months away. Time is still available to do the kind of necessary study and homework, to secure resources—order worship bulletins, etc.—and plan with those who work specifically with music, assuming they are not the same personnel as the liturgy task group.

The second of the two annual groups could go to work after the Epiphany season begins, *immediately* after if Easter comes early. Some of the same persons who took part in the Christmas group might well be present to help provide continuity with previous efforts. The new season offers its own freshness of approach. Lent, Easter, and Pentecost provide the format of this effort just as Advent, Christmas, and Epiphany were the format of the fall group.

Celebrating All Three Acts

Most Christians are amazed and excited to learn of the richness of the Christian year and how its message disturbs and comforts our own lives. As laymen take responsibility in sharing the shaping of the liturgy for the seasons, many will become aware for the first time of the contemporary power of this historic means of presenting the gospel. Their work with the meaning of the Christian year in its individual seasons informs their understanding of all worship, including the Sunday morning hour.

Christmas, for example, is often stripped of Advent and Epiphany. In many churches Easter likewise has shed Lent and Pentecost. But these two great proclamations are part of a package. Advent begins the Christian year and calls for preparation. More than a warning to "stand by," the Advent season points to who is coming and asks what it means to receive Christ when he comes. Christmas is filled with much greater meaning when Advent, Act I of this three-act drama, has been preparing the way. We examine ourselves to ask how often we turn Christ away, because we "have not ministered to the least of these, my brothers." The colors, sounds, and sense of expectation of his coming can be illustrated and proclaimed in traditional and contemporary ways. The most widely accepted Advent symbolism is a wreath with four purple candles plus a white one. Traditional Scripture lessons include the second coming and the stories of John the Baptist.

An alert liturgy group can call upon those who teach children to join forces. Like youth making a movie, the making of posters and other visual symbols can stimulate the discussion which brings out the message of the season. Boys and girls commissioned to produce art work, to be displayed in worship on the first Sunday of Advent, will need information about the meaning of the season. Their work, however, will likely be the catalyst for the rest of the project. A group of seventh-graders bogged down in an Advent poster session and caused the teacher to call for theological help. Shortly after an information session, one boy proclaimed the season well by altering a movie advertisement from an old magazine out of their resource stack. The advertisement read, "Coming Soon: *Rosemary's Baby.*" (Rosemary's baby was a symbol of the devil in the movie.) The boy had put these same words on his poster but placed a big "x" through "Rose."

Act II, Christmas, is a more powerful explosion in our lives when Advent comes to us through the dramatic and vivid presentation it deserves. Christmastide, those twelve days which begin December 25, is not likely to hold up well against our cultural pattern of dismissing the total season immediately after that day has passed. Laymen who are charged by the pastor to "put Christ back in Christmas" and to reverse society's ways and customs are in for a hard time. If we look, however, within our own services of worship and within our own church life, we can discover some deeper meanings of this celebration of the gift of Christ.

Christmas Decoration Sunday worked. The liturgy task group initiated an every-member decoration hour on the Sunday preceding Christmas Day. Instead of attending individual education classes, all persons went into a large room and put together Christmas posters, signs, door decorations, and other visual expressions of Christmas. These creations could be for home or church, and the results were about evenly divided. Such an effort not only produces helpful decorations, but it also can involve spontaneous groupings that are quite interesting—family units working together, exclusive and mixed age groups, and different levels of seriousness and fun.

Epiphany, which is Act III, must be one of the most forgotten seasons on our Christian calendar, even more so than Advent. We are a forward-looking people and have little patience with what has passed ("I'm not interested in what somebody way back there did"). We are interested in *now*. Advent is less of a problem because our society is already celebrating Christmas as soon as Thanksgiving is over, if not before. Are the first three weeks of December for Advent or Christmas? Only the Christian can tell for sure. But Epiphany—that's another story. If we can't hold still for

150

the last eleven days of Christmastide, how can we enter into Act III?

Epiphany can take on flesh and blood, however. As Advent was the preparation for Christmas, Epiphany can offer an alert liturgy group a wide choice of instruments for letting it be known that the gift of Christmas is to be manifest in our lives. We have the symbol of the Wise Men, responding to God's gift of Christ by bringing their offering and by emerging from the Gentile world, telling us that the gospel is for all people of all lands. Prayers and hymns from other nations and the various races within our own nation are a good worship beginning. Displays of photographs, prints, paintings, and various art pieces from other cultures can be put together in most congregations. The pastor who follows a lectionary or who is aware of the significance of the season is likely to be preaching about ethics and about mission—the moving into action with what God has given us.

The Second Cycle

The second big celebration cycle of the church centers in Easter. Lent-Easter-Pentecost is structured like single services of worship also. The season of Lent, which is much longer than its counterpart, Advent, has been gaining strength in Protestant churches. The liturgy group usually has more of a model to work with, including an Ash Wednesday service to announce the beginning of this season of self-examination and confession. The history of the formation of Lent into seven weeks is interesting.[1] Lenten music is more plentiful, the symbols and other resources are more abundant and offer a much wider range than can be found at Advent time.

[1] Fred D. Gealy, *Celebration* (Nashville: Graded Press, 1969), pp. 48-49.

Holy Week has not been lost in even some of the more nonliturgical churches, even if it is signaled often by a series of evangelistic services.

The liturgy task group has a rich supply of material to draw from for the Easter season. The abundance of biblical material directly related to resurrection is found throughout the New Testament. And most significant of all, the church's primary symbol comes from this event. Material about the cross is unlimited, and each year churches who open themselves in a search for new messages from it come forth with some of our most communicative liturgical forms.

Pentecost is that third act, sending us on our way again, witnessing to the Word that has been made known to us in Easter. Although it has sometimes been given over to sects in the same way we Protestants have been assigning Lent to Roman Catholics, it is on the way to recovery. Probably its low profile in our day is less an effort to ignore it and more a matter of simply not finding in it the dramatic possibilities that other seasons offer.

A Great Calling

Liturgy groups have a great calling. By helping restore the imagery and recovering the power of Act I and Act III in our two central Christian year dramas, they also remind us of the meaning and importance of the corresponding opening and closing sections in weekly worship. We need Act I, the service of confession which precedes the service of praise (sermon, Scriptures, anthem, etc.), and Act III, the service of offering following the sermon by which we openly and gladly commit ourselves to take up his cross and follow him.

Task groups for liturgy can and do operate on bases other than focusing on these two seasons and in assisting in the planning for weekly services of worship. They serve their churches in a most helpful way when they approach specific areas of worship, such as the wedding and funeral statements given earlier. As theologically oriented groups, they can search out how the Christian church has understood itself through history and does now express itself through its many approaches to confession, the affirming of its faith through creeds, or the meaning of offering in worship. Statements produced by sharp probing into such areas by the laity can make lasting contributions to these various acts of worship.

A rather different and potentially exciting task that some groups are undertaking is the creating of outdoor banners. Because of the deception in size of outdoor displays, standards sturdy enough and large enough to display good-sized banners are necessary. But efforts of this kind are well worth the trouble. A friend of mine tells of the joy of passing through a small town one Sunday morning and seeing a beautiful banner bearing the symbol of Holy Communion. It might have been a baptismal banner, a symbol of the season of the Christian year, or some other expression of the Christian faith. If no liturgy group is organized to accept responsibility of this kind, a special "outside banner" force could find here an opportunity to make an excellent contribution to the church and the community.

An important feature of worship task groups is their appointment in meeting a specific need or to do a particular job. A person who joins knows that he won't be attending meetings in which the committee has really nothing to do but which yet feels obligated to meet. He also knows that the group will be dissolved when the particular task has been completed. The high level of satisfactory results ensuing from this job-oriented approach evidences the value of the method and suggests its wide utilization.

The benefit of liturgy groups will probably vary from

zero (or worse) to extremely helpful, depending on where, when, and with whom they are tried. But their help can be most vital for the pastor as well as for the total church. They provide the pastor with views other than his own and provide them from the very people for whom the worship is planned. A minister's mood or his favorite approach is countered by a wider base. One man just can't come up with as many ideas and constructive views as can a group. And he develops colleagues in knowledge and concern about worship who can do things and communicate understandings through channels not open to him.

The congregation can benefit in at least the following ways: (1) the task group makes possible the deepening of their own devotional lives and the lives of others in the congregation by their better understanding of the meaning of liturgy; (2) those who have been involved in the planning and work are far more likely to enter into the celebration on Sunday morning; (3) the presence of a nucleus of people who already know what is planned for a service of worship can be invaluable, especially if some parts of the service represent major changes from the past.

Who Is in Charge Here?

The role of the pastor varies in congregations, but most pastors become concerned when laymen begin dealing with the services of worship. No intelligent pastor wants to have the services put together by popular vote, especially knowing that this can be a pooling of ignorance. But most laymen who are not looking for a place to grind their ax are not the least bit eager to take over the total services of worship. They are, for the most part, aware that their limitations of knowledge and training are usually greater than those of a pastor who is interested enough in worship to encourage a task group to participate in it. Even the best informed have probably gathered most of their liturgical information from the pastor. They also suspect that the many details, adjustments, and other unexpected factors require one person to be able to act at times without a committee meeting.

Laymen whose primary concern is a desire to learn about worship and to manifest this learning in the church's service have no difficulty in acknowledging the need for the pastor to have a final say in most matters. Leaving the service of worship to popular vote is only a little more preferable than taking a vote on the content and delivery of the sermon. Rather than discouraging a group, this understanding of roles enables them to express themselves freely in the meetings. If the total task group disagrees with the pastor, both need to give the point more consideration. If serious conflict is always existing between the pastor and the task group, then the liturgical problem will undoubtedly be a symptom of a much more serious problem.

Granting the pastor this kind of authority is a way of saying that we the laity have charged you with the responsibility of providing leadership. When this leadership is not satisfactory or when laymen are not seriously concerned to contribute to the planning and background of the liturgy, the time is at hand for deep conversation about the basic meaning of clergy and laity—and about the meaning of Christian worship.

An awakening is taking place in the services of worship of local churches. It is an awakening of *Christian* worship when it is a combined effort of both clergy and laity, when it takes seriously both its content and its communication, and when it is understood as the most serious work the church has before it today.

Some Basic Books on Worship

Cullmann, Oscar, *Early Christian Worship*. Trans. by A. Stewart Todd and James B. Torrance. London: SCM Press, 1953.

Delling, Gerhard. *Worship in the New Testament*. Trans. by Percy Scott. Philadelphia: The Westminster Press, 1962.

Dix, Dom Gregory. *The Shape of the Liturgy*. London: Dacre Press, 1945.

Gealy, Fred D. *Celebration*. Nashville: Graded Press, 1969.

Hammond, Peter. *Liturgy and Architecture*. London: Barrie and Rockliff, 1960.

Hoon, Paul Waitman. *The Integrity of Worship*. Nashville: Abingdon Press, 1971.

Jungmann, Josef, S.J. *The Liturgy of the World*. Trans. by H. E. Winstone. Collegeville, Minn.: The Liturgical Press, 1966.

Robinson, John A. T. *Liturgy Coming to Life*. Philadelphia: The Westminster Press, 1960.

Shepherd, Massey H., Jr. *At All Times and in All Places*. 3rd. ed. rev. New York: The Seabury Press, 1965.

Thompson, Bard. *Liturgies of the Western Church*. Cleveland: World Publishing Company, 1961.

White, James F. *New Forms of Worship*. Nashville: Abingdon Press, 1971.